Jannah

Home at Last

OMAR
SULEIMAN

KUBE
PUBLISHING

In association with
YAQEEN™
INSTITUTE FOR ISLAMIC RESEARCH

Jannah: Home at Last

First published in England by
Kube Publishing Ltd
Markfield Conference Centre
Ratby Lane, Markfield
Leicestershire, LE67 9SY
United Kingdom

Tel: +44 (0) 1530 249230
Website: www.kubepublishing.com
Email: info@kubepublishing.com

Cataloguing-in-Publication Data is available from the British Library.

ISBN 978-1-84774-230-8 Casebound
eISBN 978-1-84774-231-5 Ebook

Proofreading and editing: Wordsmiths
Cover design, typesetting and Arabic calligraphy: Jannah Haque
Printed by: IMAK Ofset, Turkey.

Transliteration Guide

A brief guide to some of the letters and symbols used in the Arabic transliteration in this book.

th	ث	*ḥ*	ح	*dh*	ذ
ṣ	ص	*ḍ*	ض	*ṭ*	ط
ẓ	ظ	ʿ	ع	ʾ	ء
ā	ـَا آ	*ī*	ـِي	*ū*	ـُو

صلى الله عليه وسلم May the peace and blessings of Allah be upon him.	عز وجل Glorified and Majestic (is He).	رضي الله عنه May Allah be pleased with him.
رضي الله عنها May Allah be pleased with her.	رضي الله عنهما May Allah be pleased with them both.	رحمهما الله May Allah bless them both.
عليه السلام May peace be upon him.	عليها السلام May peace be upon her.	عليهما السلام May peace be upon them both.

Contents

Welcome to Your Eternal Home

Prelude

Jannah–Home at Last

The material state of this *dunyā* (temporal world) is heavily stratified, with the majority of the world's population living in poverty whilst the uber-rich thrive in lofty mansions and spend their wealth lavishly. Against this abysmal backdrop, the good life appears to be defined through purely material standards. But the wise person sees through this mirage and realises that the current values of materialism and hedonism only delay the inevitable truth that we will all die and be placed in graves beneath the earth. It is at this moment one will be forced to meet their Maker, Who will decree whether a person will spend their eternal otherworldly life in Paradise or the Hellfire.

The true believer is cognisant of these metaphysical truths, and as a result, is able to bear the difficulties of the present world with relative ease. This worldly life is nothing more than a test, and if a person lives a life strictly defined by the values of monotheism and acceptance of the Final Prophet ﷺ, they will be welcomed in the permanent abode of bliss: Jannah. If one fully internalises this fact, they will not be perturbed by the anxieties and perplexities of this world, for they know that Allah will handsomely reward them for every virtuous act or supplication that they make to Him.

There is an eternal abode of happiness that is waiting for you. But in order to enter it, you must activate it with your deeds. This work will provide the spiritual resources to ensure this process can be executed successfully. Salvation is within reach.

ادْخُلُوهَا بِسَلَامٍ آمِنِينَ

(It will be said to the believers)

"Enter (Jannah) in peace and security."

AL-ḤIJR, 46

1

Jannah is Waiting For You

After leading the Fajr prayer on one given morning, the Prophet ﷺ did something peculiar: he began to stretch his hand out in the air, as if he was trying to pluck something metaphysical or incorporeal. During this fascinating sight, the Prophet ﷺ was smiling profusely. Eventually, however, the Prophet retracted his hand and resumed his normal state. This sight attracted the attention of the Companions رضي الله عنهم, who turned to the Prophet ﷺ and asked: "On this day, we found you doing something that we have never seen you do before. It was as if you stretched your hand out and were trying to pluck something. But then you suddenly pulled your hand back." The Prophet ﷺ addressed the query of the Companions رضي الله عنهم by stating:

إِنِّي رَأَيْتُ الجَنَّةَ فَتَنَاوَلْتُ مِنْهَا عُنْقُودًا وَلَو أَخَذْتُه لأَكَلْتُمْ مِّنْهُ مَا بَقِيَتِ الدُّنْيَا

"I just saw Paradise and happened to glance at some of the grapes from it. Had I plucked them, you would have eaten from them as long as the world lasted."

The Prophet ﷺ then concluded his explanation by stating: "But then I saw the Hellfire, so I pulled my hand away from it."

Imagine if every one of us had the opportunity to directly see both Paradise and the Hellfire in front of them; such a privilege would undoubtedly play a role in shifting our behaviour and actions. However, merely seeing something is not enough to bring forth change. Instead, the key decisive factor is being able to perceive it and appreciate its gravity. The Prophet ﷺ alluded to this very psychological fact when he said:

الجَنَّةُ أَقْرَبُ إِلَى أَحَدِكُمْ مِنْ شِرَاكِ نَعْلِيه، وَالنَّارُ كَذلِك

"Paradise is nearer to you than the laces of your shoes, and the same is the case for the Hellfire."

From this powerful Hadith, we derive the important spiritual reality that Paradise is currently present before us and within reach. We should always be conscious of this fact and proceed to enter it right now spiritually with our hearts and minds. If we fail to capitalise on this reality, then the gates of Paradise might be closed before us, thereby preventing us from accessing it in the Hereafter.

In an important and powerful report, the Prophet ﷺ said:

لَمَّا خَلَقَ اللَّهُ الْجَنَّةَ قَالَ لِجِبْرِيلَ: اذْهَبْ فَانْظُرْ إِلَيْهَا

"Immediately after Allah created Paradise, He called Jibrīl and said to him: 'Go and look at it (to see what I have arranged for its inhabitants).'"

Jibrīl ﷺ obeyed his Creator's command and enjoyed the golden opportunity of being the first entity in the Universe to directly witness the delights of Paradise. After setting his sights on the stunning plane of beauty that awaited the believers, Jibrīl ﷺ went to his Creator and exclaimed:

أَيْ رَبِّ وَعِزَّتِكَ لَا يَسْمَعُ بِهَا أَحَدٌ إِلَّا دَخَلَهَا

"O my Lord, by Your glory, no one shall hear of it except that they will enter it."

By this statement, Jibrīl ﷺ was expressing his astonishment at the wonders and glories found in Paradise, and his initial belief that every person would aim to enter it after being informed of its endless bounties. However, his initial impression was challenged after Allah ﷻ placed a number of hardships and obstacles in the path to Paradise. After these difficulties and stressors were put in place, Allah ﷻ addressed Jibrīl ﷺ by stating: "Now go and look at it again." Jibrīl ﷺ followed the order of his Lord and looked at Paradise once more. After laying his sights on the obstacle-ridden path to Paradise, Jibrīl returned to his Lord and said: "O my Lord,

When a Muslim asks Allah for Paradise three times, Paradise responds, "O Allah, grant him entrance to Paradise." And when he seeks refuge from the Hellfire from Allah, Hellfire says, "O Allah, give him refuge (from the Fire)." Both of them wish good for the believer.

I now fear that no one will be able to enter it." This marked a complete retraction from his earlier response.

Allah ﷻ then addressed Jibrīl ﵇ by stating: "Go and look at the Hellfire and see what I have arranged for its people." Jibrīl ﵇ went to the Hellfire and laid his sights on its horrors. He returned to his Lord and said:

أيْ رَبِّ وَعِزَّتِكَ لَا يَسْمَعُ بِهَا أَحَدٌ فَيَدْخُلُهَا

"O Lord, by Your might, no one shall hear of this place and then proceed to enter it."

With this declaration, Jibrīl ﵇ was alluding to the terrors and perils found in the plane of damnation, and how no being would wish to enter it after being informed of its nature. However, Allah ﷻ corrected this assumption of Jibrīl and said to him: "Now go and look at it again." Jibrīl ﵇ returned to the path of the Hellfire and found that it was now surrounded with vain pleasures, comforts, and desires. After laying his sights on this new state, he returned to Allah and said: "O my Lord, I now fear that no one will be able to avoid it." After hearing this response, Allah ﷻ turned to Jannah and said: "Speak, O Jannah." In response, Jannah said:

قَدْ أَفْلَحَ ٱلْمُؤْمِنُون

"Successful indeed are the believers."[1]

---

1 *al-Mu'minūn*, 1.

After hearing this recital, Jibrīl ﷺ and the rest of the Angels responded to Paradise's declaration by stating:

طُوبَى لَك مَنزِلُ المُلُوك

"Glad tidings and blessings to you, for you are the home of kings."

Yet, the inhabitants of Paradise are not worldly kings who ruled a certain principality or state in this Earth. Instead, the word "king" here alludes to how the believers attain the status of kings and queens by demonstrating sincere obedience to their Creator, Allah ﷻ. In another relevant Hadith, the Prophet ﷺ mentioned that Paradise and Hell engaged in a verbal dispute with one another in the presence of their Lord. During this heated exchange, Paradise said:

مَا لِي لاَ يَدْخُلُنِي إِلَّا ضُعَفَاءُ النَّاسِ وَسَقَطُهُم

"(My Lord) why is it the case that no one save the weak individuals and the downtrodden enter inside me?"

In the same moment, the Hellfire turned to its Creator ﷻ, saying:

أُوثِرْتُ بالمُتَكَبِّرِينَ، والْمُتَجَبِّرِينَ

"(My Lord) why is it that only the arrogant (al-mutakabbirīn) and the proud ones (al-mutajabbirīn) enter inside me?"

Allah ﷻ then addressed Paradise and said:

أَنْتِ رَحْمَتِي أَرْحَمُ بِكِ مَنْ أَشَاءُ مِنْ عِبَادِي

"You are My mercy whereby I am merciful to whomever I wish amongst My slaves."

Thereafter, Allah ﷻ will turn to the Hellfire and address its point of contention by stating: "And you are My mode of punishment, whereby I will punish whomever I wish through you." After hearing this set of responses from their Lord, the two will wait in deep anticipation for the Day of Judgement to occur to see who will be blessed with a life of infinite bliss, and who will be cursed with a life of infinite damnation. In fact, whenever you happen to make a *du'ā'* (supplication) that references either one of them, both will almost immediately respond and call to their Creator. In one key Hadith, the Prophet ﷺ said:

مَا مِنْ يَومٍ إِلَّا وَالجَنَّةُ وَالنَّارُ يَسْأَلَان

"There is no day that passes by except that both Paradise and Hellfire ask Allah (about their inhabitants)."

In the same report, the Prophet ﷺ related that Paradise makes the following supplication on a daily basis:

يَا رَبِّ قَدْ طَابَ ثَمَرِيْ وَاطَّرَدَتْ أَنْهَارِيْ وَاشْتَقْتُ إِلَى أَوْلِيَائِيْ فَعَجِّلْ إِلَي بِأَهْلِيْ

"O my Lord, my fruits have become ripe and my rivers are flowing. I can hardly wait to see my close friends. So, hasten the arrival of my people."

In a parallel fashion, the Hellfire calls to its Lord and states:

اشْتَدَّ حَرِّي وَبَعُدَ قَعْرِي وَعَظُمَ جَمْرِي، عَجِّلْ إِلَهِي إِلَيَّ بِأَهْلِي

"O my Lord, my heat has intensified, my abyss has reached the furthest depth, and my flames and embers are glowing with fury. So, hasten the arrival of my people."

From this report a number of spiritual and religious benefits may be derived. Perhaps the key point that can be deduced from this Hadith is that in their respective supplications, both Paradise and Hell are concerned with the wellbeing of the pious believers and the righteous. This is proven by the following Hadith of the Prophet ﷺ, which is found in the *Musnad* of Imam Aḥmad:

مَا سَأَلَ رَجُلٌ مُسْلِمٌ الجَنَّةَ ثَلَاثَ مَرَّاتٍ قَطُّ إِلَّا قَالَتِ الجَنَّةُ: اللَّهُمَّ أَدْخِلْهُ الجَنَّةَ؛ وَلَا اسْتَجَارَ مِنَ النَّارِ إِلَّا قَالَتِ النَّارُ: اللَّهُمَّ أَجِرْهُ

"No Muslim person asks for Paradise three times except that Paradise responds and says, 'O Allah, grant him entrance to Paradise.' And he does not seek refuge from the Hellfire except that the Hellfire says, 'O Allah, give him refuge (from the Fire).'"

If one were to truly know the pleasures of Paradise, then no degree of pleasure or pain in this world would be able to adversely affect their pursuit of that permanent abode of happiness. Paradise cannot wait to receive you but how eager are you in exerting your religious efforts to attain it?

Thus, whilst both of them wish good for the believer, it is Paradise that is the most eager in welcoming the beloved believers and submitters to the true faith. In another pertinent report, the noble Successor Kaʿb al-Aḥbār ﷀ related that every time Allah ﷻ gazes at Paradise, He addresses it by saying to it:

طِيبِي لِأَهْلِكِ

"Adorn and beautify yourself for your people."

As such, every time it is viewed by its Creator, Paradise amplifies its beauty and splendour. This process will continue until the Day of Judgement, which will mark the end of time and culminate with the eternal salvation of the believers. Upon examining the various reports and narrations found in the Prophetic Sunnah, one will find that Paradise's love for the believers is amplified in certain time periods and contexts. For instance, Paradise not only loves the sacred month of Ramadan, but it celebrates it as its favourite season. In an oft-cited Hadith, it is authentically established that the Prophet ﷺ said:

إِذا جَاءَ رَمَضَانُ، فُتِّحَتْ أَبْوَابُ الجَنَّةِ، وغُلِّقَت أَبْوَابُ النَّارِ، وصُفِّدتِ الشياطِينُ

"When the month of Ramadan commences, the gates of Paradise are fully opened, and the gates of the Hellfire are firmly closed, and the devils are put in chains."

This beautiful report serves as an acute reminder that during every night of this sacred month, the doors of Paradise are opened to the widest extent possible, an event which signifies the amplified mercy of Allah during this special period. If a Muslim capitalises on this period and worships their Lord sincerely, their spot in Paradise will be even further beautified.

Paradise cannot wait to receive you and welcome you with open arms. But you now must ask yourself the most important question of your life: how eager are you to receive it? If you fail to exert your best religious efforts in attaining Paradise, you are essentially jeopardising your salvation in the Hereafter. The Prophet ﷺ stressed this point in a noteworthy report:

يَا قَوْمُ اطْلُبُوا الْجَنَّةَ جَهْدَكُمْ، وَاهْرَبُوا مِنَ النَّارِ جَهْدَكُمْ ، فَإِنَّ الْجَنَّةَ لَا يَنَامُ طَالِبُهَا، وَإِنَّ النَّارَ لَا يَنَامُ هَارِبُهَا، أَلَا إِنَّ الْآخِرَةَ الْيَوْمَ مُحَفَّفَةٌ بِالْمَكَارِهِ، وَإِنَّ الدُّنْيَا مُحَفَّفَةٌ بِالشَّهَوَاتِ

"O my people! Seek Paradise with all that you have, and flee from the Hellfire with all that you have. This is the case since the seeker of Paradise does not sleep, nor does the fleer of the Fire. But indeed, the Hereafter is surrounded with difficulties, and verily the transient world is surrounded with base pleasures."

However, if one were to know the pleasures of Paradise, then no degree of pleasure or pain in this world would be able to adversely affect their pursuit of the permanent abode of happiness. For instance, when the Prophet ﷺ witnessed the bunch of grapes, nothing from the worldly dimension or his surroundings could affect his thoughts or pleasant sensations. Similarly, in this regard one may consider the story of Āsiyah ﵂, the wife of the wicked tyrant Firʿawn.

Whilst she was being brutally tortured by her husband owing to her faith in Allah, Āsiyah ﷺ was smiling. The reason for her pleasure was that Allah was metaphysically presenting her eminent palace in Paradise before her very eyes. No degree of torture or punishment could rob her of her happiness. Thus, before one can actually enter Paradise in the eternal realm found in the other world, they must first exert their best and most sincere efforts to attain it in this temporal domain. This explains why the sincere believers are greeted with the following call after they pass away and move on to the permanent realm:

يَٰٓأَيَّتُهَا ٱلنَّفْسُ ٱلْمُطْمَئِنَّةُ ٱرْجِعِىٓ إِلَىٰ رَبِّكِ رَاضِيَةً مَّرْضِيَّةً
فَٱدْخُلِى فِى عِبَٰدِى وَٱدْخُلِى جَنَّتِى

"[Allah will say to the righteous:] 'O tranquil soul! Return to your Lord, well pleased and well pleasing. So, join My servants, and enter My Paradise.'"[2]

[2] *al-Fajr*, 27–30.

2

The Moment You Enter Jannah

The believers will not enter Paradise at the same time, route, or manner. Whilst it is true that they will enter through different gates and be assigned various ranks and privileges, every single inhabitant of Paradise will be pleased due to their attainment of the abode of bliss. However, during their time on this Earth, the true believer is not only committed to attaining Paradise, but they also exert their sincerest efforts to enter it with the least degree of accountability and the highest rank in the Hereafter. A person who is instilled with such a mode of thinking is said to have a "Jannah mindset". Such an individual views every single second in this world as a golden opportunity to enter Paradise in the next world through the best gate, and without undergoing any ordeal or difficulties. This latter point is crucial, since the people of Paradise will be granted their place at different time points: whilst some will be indulging in the pleasures of their palaces, other believers will still be required to pass certain accountability tests or settle outstanding scores with other individuals.

Concerning this matter, the Prophet ﷺ said that there is a specific gate in Paradise which is assigned to individuals who will not be required to undergo any tests or trials. In the same report, the Prophet ﷺ explained that the gate in question is known as Bāb al-Ayman (The Right-Hand Gate). The Hadith concludes by stating that the rest of the people of Paradise will be required to enter the Garden of Bliss through the other gates, which do not provide the same benefits or privileges. Through this report, we learn that it is Allah ﷻ Who determines the allotment of ranks and grades in the Hereafter, and that the believers will not enter Paradise in a sequential manner. In fact, in another Hadith, the Prophet ﷺ indicated that a special class of the believers will be given the golden opportunity to enter Paradise first: the poor and the downtrodden. Moreover, they will represent the majority population of Jannah. Such a fact at first sight may oppose our preliminary intuitions, since in this world, it is the rich and the well-to-do who are always at the forefront and provided the most eminent of positions. The poor, on the other hand, are either delayed excessively or shunned altogether. But our religion teaches us that if one wishes to enter Paradise through its express avenue, then they must emulate the poor.

However, this is not a universal rule that applies to all individuals. For instance, the noble Companion Abū Bakr al-Ṣiddīq ﷺ was wealthy in relative terms, yet he will be one of the forerunners of Paradise. From this fact, the scholars inferred that if a person uses their wealth and earnings in an ethical and religiously-conscious manner, they will still be assigned a high rank in Paradise. However, the impoverished and downtrodden will still attain a higher position in the permanent abode of bliss, since they are freed from the trappings and tests that are associated with wealth.

There are other qualities and characteristics which will improve one's prospects of being from amongst the first people to enter Paradise. For instance, in a Hadith recorded in the *Muʿjam* of Imam al-Ṭabarānī it is related that the Prophet ﷺ said:

أَوَّلُ مَنْ يُدْعَى إِلَى الجَنَّةِ الحَمَّادُونَ: الَّذِينَ يَحْمَدُونَ اللهَ فِي السَّرَّاءِ وَالضَّرَّاءِ

"The first of people to be called to Paradise are the ḥammādūn: they are the ones who praise Allah during times of ease and difficulty."

This Hadith indicates that a person's rank and position in Paradise has little to do with one's personal possessions and wealth, and is in fact tied to how one utilises their privileges to attain the pleasure of their Creator, regardless of their circumstances. Thus, a person must carefully reflect on whether or not they are making effective use of their current state of affairs to serve their religion and attain Paradise, since that will determine how quickly they will enter the abode of bliss and their rank.

Another important and related topic worthy of exploration is how the believers will wait outside the gates of Paradise. In a Hadith, the Prophet ﷺ mentioned that the believers will be situated under a tree that is in close proximity to Paradise. The tree will be surrounded by two flowing rivers; the believers will drink from one of them and bathe from the other. This cleansing process will purify them from all forms of spiritual filth, and they will all be shining with a brilliant and marvelous light. The Prophet ﷺ then mentioned that as the believers wait in this plane, they will observe the gates of Paradise and Hell, which number eight and seven respectively. Such a sight will undoubtedly instil serenity and tranquility in the hearts of the believers, since it will be read as a confirmation that Allah's mercy overcomes His wrath. The Prophet ﷺ specifically mentioned the distinguishing features of the gates of Paradise, and what noble acts allow one to enter through them. Amongst the titles mentioned in this regard were the gates of *ṣalāh* (prayer), jihad (striving for the sake of Allah), *ṣadaqah* (voluntary charity), and *ṣiyām* (fasting). The Prophet ﷺ then mentioned that the gate of fasting is known as Bāb al-Rayyān (The Gate of Quenching Thirst), which can only be traversed by those who were exceptional in their fasting. Upon hearing these astonishing facts, the preeminent Companion Abū Bakr al-Ṣiddīq رضي الله عنه addressed the Prophet ﷺ by saying: "Will there be any person who will be called from all the gates?" The Prophet ﷺ issued the following response to the query of Abū Bakr ؓ:

نَعَمْ، وَأَرْجُو أَنْ تَكُونَ مِنْهُمْ

"Yes, and I hope that you will be one of them."

This response from the Prophet ﷺ is no matter of surprise, since Abū Bakr ؓ was known to be exemplary in every one of these acts of worship. However, the majority of people lack such exertion, and can only excel in one of these categories at best; they can thus only hope to enter Paradise through a single door. Allah is aware of the deficiencies of His servants, and for this reason, He has provided us a variety of means to have these gates opened, despite our deficiencies and imperfections. For instance, in an important Hadith concerning the virtues of the *wuḍū'* (ritual ablution), it is established that the Prophet ﷺ said:

مَا مِنْ مُسْلِمٍ يَتَوَضَّأُ فَيُحْسِنُ الوُضُوءَ ثُمَّ يَقُولُ: أَشْهَدُ أَنْ لَا إِلَهَ إِلَّا اللهُ وَأَشْهَدُ أَنَّ مُحَمَّدًا عَبْدُهُ وَرَسُولُهُ إِلَّا فُتِحَتْ لَهُ ثَمَانِيَةُ أَبْوَابِ الجَنَّةِ يَدْخُلُ مِنْ أَيِّهَا شَاءَ

"There is no Muslim who performs wuḍū' excellently and then says, 'I bear witness that there is no god except Allah and that Muhammad is His servant and Messenger', except that all eight gates of Paradise will be opened for him and he shall enter through any one of them that he wishes."

However, it is important to mention that even this virtue is not attained merely by reciting the supplication after performing any type of ablution. Instead, the Hadith mentions that the

Believers will enter Jannah through different gates and will be assigned various ranks and privileges. The true believer is not only committed to attaining Paradise, but they also exert their sincerest efforts to enter it with the least degree of accountability and the highest rank in the Hereafter.

person must perform the *wuḍū'* meticulously whilst fulfilling all its conditions and pillars. This can only be achieved by someone who is well attentive of their *ṣalāh* and consistently ensures that it is performed with proper care. Conversely, a person who is lackadaisical with their prayer will likewise not be cautious and observant when making their daily ablutions. Such a fact explains why the Prophet ﷺ said that if a person's prayers are correctly executed and in order, then all their other affairs and deeds will be deemed satisfactory as well when they are weighed on the Scale. This discussion concerning the various categories and names of the gates of Paradise logically leads to another question: what is their nature and dimensions? In a report, the Companion ʿAlī ibn Abī Ṭālib ؓ mentioned that these gates are arranged vertically—and not horizontally—whereby one is above the other. This divinely-set arrangement of the gates in this manner is to illustrate that the prominently-positioned gates are more virtuous than the lower ones.

The ummah of the Prophet ﷺ will be blessed with its own monumental gate, through which every Muslim believer will pass to enter Paradise. In an authentic tradition, the Prophet ﷺ stated that the gate which the members of his ummah will traverse exceeds the distance that a rider travels over the course of several years. In another report, the Prophet ﷺ stated that the spatial extent of his ummah's gate is commensurate to the distance between the Arabian cities of Hajar and Mecca. Other reports invoke the names of other cities, but the upshot is the same: in terms of its dimensions and size, the gate of the Muslim nation will be breathtaking. Despite the astonishing width of this gate, the Prophet ﷺ mentioned that the shoulders of the Muslims walking through the gate will be compressed against one another.

In an astonishing and remarkable narration, the Prophet ﷺ said:

أَتَانِي جِبْرِيلُ فَأَخَذَ بِيَدَيَّ فَأَرَانِي بَابَ الْجَنَّةِ الَّذِي تَدْخُلُ مِنْهُ أُمَّتِي

"Jibrīl came to me, held my hand, and showed me the gate through which my ummah is going to enter Paradise."

Upon hearing this, the noble Companion Abū Bakr ؓ exclaimed to the Prophet ﷺ:

يَا رَسُولَ اللَّهِ، وَدِدْتُ أَنِّي كُنْتُ مَعَكَ حَتَّى أَنْظُرَ إِلَيْهِ

"O Messenger of Allah, I would love to be with you such that I may see it (i.e., the gate)."

In response to his wish, the Prophet ﷺ said:

أَمَا إِنَّكَ يَا أَبَا بَكْرٍ أَوَّلُ مَنْ يَدْخُلُ الْجَنَّةَ مِنْ أُمَّتِي

"As for you, O Abū Bakr, you shall be the first member of my ummah to enter Paradise."

The Prophet ﷺ also gave glad tidings to the rest of his ummah as well by addressing them all with the following statement: "You are the best of nations since you are the final one to come. Yet, you are the first amongst them to enter Paradise." From this statement, one infers that the Messenger of Allah ﷺ will be first Prophet to enter Paradise, and in honour of his great status, his ummah will be the first of nations to enter the permanent abode of bliss. As such, the Muslim ummah will stand behind the Prophet ﷺ and await his advancement towards the gate of Paradise. The great Successor Qatādah ﵀ mentioned that this sight would be momentous, as the Muslims will be able to see the bounties of Paradise through its gates. The Prophet ﷺ would then proceed towards the gate and then ring a bell, which will signify to the Keeper (*Khāzin*) of Paradise that the inhabitants of Paradise have arrived. In a Hadith, this momentous event is described with the following statement: "I will be the first person to hold the chain of Paradise and clatter it, and I am not boasting." The Keeper of Paradise will approach the Prophet ﷺ and say:

مَنْ أَنْتَ

"Who are you?"

The Prophet ﷺ will then say: "Muhammad." In response, the Angel will welcome the Prophet ﷺ and exclaim:

بِكَ أُمِرْتُ أَلَّا أَفْتَحَ لِأَحَدٍ قَبْلَكَ

"I was ordered to not open this for anyone before you."

In order to enter Paradise, every Muslim will have to attain its key, which in metaphysical terms consists of the *shahādah* (testimony of faith) of *lā ilāha illa Allāh* (there is no God but Allah). But merely verbalising the *shahādah* on one's tongue is insufficient; the scholars point out that the operation of the key can only be actualised if it has teeth, which are pious deeds.

Thus, the shape and effectiveness of our key depends on our deeds and our station in the sight of Allah. Moreover, in another Hadith reported on the authority of Salmān al-Fārisī ☙, the Prophet ﷺ mentioned that the believers will be provided passports in order to guarantee their safe passage across the Ṣirāṭ (Bridge):

إِنَّ اللهَ عَزَّ وَجَلَّ يُعْطِي الْمُؤْمِنَ جَوَازًا عَلَى الصِّرَاطِ: بِسْمِ اللهِ الرَّحْمَنِ الرَّحِيمِ
هَذَا كِتَابٌ مِنَ الْعَزِيزِ الْحَكِيمِ

*"Indeed, Allah Most High will give the believer a passport
on the Ṣirāṭ [which will bear the following message]:
'In the name of Allah, the Possessor of mercy and the
Bestower of mercy. This is a letter of assurance from
the All-Powerful and the Most Wise.'"*

In the same letter, Allah will issue the following order:

أَدْخِلُوهُ جَنَّةً عَالِيَةً قُطُوفُهَا دَانِيَةٌ

*"Allow this person to enter Paradise with all of its loftiness
and with its fruits within reach."*

Thus, on the Day of Judgement, the believer will not only be provided with a key, but they will also be given a passport. What happens next is beautifully described in the Qur'an:

حَتَّىٰ إِذَا جَآءُوهَا وَفُتِحَتْ أَبْوَٰبُهَا

"...and then they come and its gates are slowly opened..."[3]

---

3 *Zumar*, 73.

This verse indicates that as the believers are led to the gates of Paradise, their doors will be opened for them as they near the entrance area. In his exegetical writings, Imam Ibn Qayyim al-Jawziyyah ﵀ mentions that there is a significant difference in how the inhabitants of Paradise and Hell will reach their respective destinations. To illustrate this point, he draws to our attention the verse that mentions how the inhabitants of the Hellfire will be transported:

حَتَّىٰٓ إِذَا جَآءُوهَا فُتِحَتْ أَبْوَٰبُهَا

"...as soon as they get to it, the gates will be suddenly opened..."[4]

The inhabitants of Hellfire will then be immediately thrown into the Hellfire. The wording and import of this verse are different from that of the positive reception that will be provided to the believers. The latter will arrive at the entrance of Paradise and the gates will slowly open, thereby exhibiting the beauty of the gardens in a gradual and thought-evoking manner. To further amplify the pleasantness of the experience, the believers will enter Paradise as collective groups (*zumar*). The existence of groups is a special element since it mirrors the collectiveness that is found in many special events, such as the Hajj pilgrimage, the two Eids, and congregational prayer. But the bliss and happiness found in the otherworldly gathering will be undoubtedly greater, since this will be the greatest assembly of the believers ever recorded in history. Moreover, in the front line of the

---

[4] Zumar, 71.

gathering the Prophet ﷺ, his noble Companions ﷺ, and his pure household will be present. At this point, one may ask what acts or deeds they may perform to improve their prospects for being a part of this blessed gathering. The answer to this question can be found in a monumental Hadith recorded in *Ṣaḥīḥ Ibn Ḥibbān*:

إِنَّ مَلَكًا بِبَابٍ مِنْ أَبْوَابِ الجَنَّةِ يَقُولُ: مَنْ يُقْرِضِ اليَوْمَ يُجْزَ غَدًا، وَمَلَكٌ بِبَابٍ آخَرَ يَقُولُ: اللَّهُمَّ أَعْطِ مُنْفِقًا خَلَفًا وَأَعْطِ مُمْسِكًا تَلَفًا

"Verily there is an Angel at a gate amongst the gates of Paradise, saying: 'Whoever gives a good loan today shall be rewarded for it tomorrow.' And then an Angel from another gate calls out and says: 'O Allah, give back more to the one who gives, and give destruction to the one who withholds.'"

These two Angels are constantly making calls and appeals to us from the highest plane conceivable: the gates of Paradise. We will only be able to benefit from their supplications by providing aid and succour to the weak and destitute in this world. One can only imagine how many times the great and noble Companion Abū Bakr responded to these calls by giving material support to the poor people in this world. For every unit of good he will be handsomely rewarded in the Hereafter. The key question is whether or not we possess the same level of eagerness to follow our pious predecessors in good and attain the blessing of entering Paradise through one of its eminent gates.

3

Your Appearance in Jannah

The Day of Judgement will be characterised with many moments of darkness and gloom, an event which will petrify many of the sons of Adam عليه السلام during their already-horrific ordeal. But Allah will provide succour to the believers by causing their good deeds to brighten their bodies as a glowing *nūr* (light). This will allow the Muslims to identify their surroundings and navigate in dangerous planes, such as the Ṣirāṭ (Bridge). But once the believers enter Paradise, a natural question which arises is what will happen to their light once its utility becomes non-existent. The scholars mention that after entering Paradise, this remaining *nūr* on their bodies will serve as an additional layer of *zīnah* (adornment) that will further beautify their forms before all onlookers. Thus, whilst a person in Paradise no longer requires any light to see their surroundings, the glittering traces of these good deeds will remain on their body forever. Of course, it is important to note that the intensity of this brightness will vary from person to person, since not every believer's deeds will be of the same value and quality. Nevertheless, the light that every person will emit will undoubtedly be spectacular. In an authentic Hadith, the Prophet ﷺ eloquently explained how the luminescence of the faces of the believers will be commensurate to the level of their *īmān* (faith). More specifically, he mentioned that the first group of people to enter Paradise will have faces that are like the full moon. In fact, even during his time in this world, the Prophet ﷺ was described as having a beautiful face that resembled the full Moon.

Taking these aforementioned points into consideration, it becomes evident that the form of the believers will be different in Paradise. In one noteworthy Hadith, the Prophet ﷺ states: "The people of Paradise will be raised in the form of Adam, 33 years of age, free of any hair on their bodies, and with kohl smeared on their eyes." This report indicates that the bodies and forms of the believers will undergo a number of deep-cutting transformations. For instance, in this worldly life there is nothing *prima facie* to suggest that bodily hair is unappealing or unattractive, especially in the case of the beard. Yet, this report serves as a reminder that the eternal plane is different, and as such our bodies, will be subject to a number of amendments. After carefully gauging some narrations

On the Day of Judgement, in moments of darkness, Allah will allow the good deeds of the believers to brighten their bodies as glowing light to navigate the path. In Paradise, the glittering traces of these good deeds will remain on their bodies forever as an additional layer of adornment.

regarding the state of the believers in Paradise, it can be inferred that they will endure as translucent or semi-corporeal beings. With reference to height and stature, the Prophet ﷺ issued the following statement: "Everyone who enters Paradise will be in the form of Adam, whose height is 60 cubits." In modern units, this would be approximately 90 feet or 30 metres. Such a level of stature will be undoubtedly astonishing and exceed the customary dimensions of this world. But the believers will undoubtedly be pleased with their new characteristics, since they will all be conferred the utmost degree of beauty and luminescence. Moreover, there will be equality in terms of age, for in an authentic tradition the Prophet ﷺ stated that all the people of Paradise will be 33 years of age. The number 33 has a unique value in the Islamic tradition. In fact, according to some Qur'anic commentators, it is the peak age of maturity that is being alluded to in the following verse:

وَلَمَّا بَلَغَ أَشُدَّهُ وَاسْتَوَىٰ آتَيْنَاهُ حُكْمًا وَعِلْمًا

"And when he reached his maturity and became perfect, We gave him wisdom and knowledge."[5]

Of course, it is important note that within the plane of Paradise, this age will not be fraught with the limitations and imperfections that are embedded within it in this *dunyā* (temporal world). Instead, it will be a number that reflects the highest level of joy and happiness. As such, the community of the believers will enter the eternal garden of bliss with

[5] *al-Qaṣaṣ*, 14.

the height of the Prophet Adam 🕊, the handsomeness of Prophet Yūsuf 🕊, and the age of Prophet ʿĪsā 🕊. And upon entering their destination, they will seek the companionship of the final Prophet of humankind, Muhammad 🕊. A famous and somewhat humorous Hadith exists concerning the age of the entrants of Paradise, wherein the Prophet 🕊 playfully gave glad tidings of Paradise to an old woman. In this report, the old woman went to the Prophet 🕊 and asked him to pray for her entry into Paradise. The Prophet 🕊 replied to her plea by stating, "But old women shall not enter Paradise." Upon hearing this, the woman began to cry profusely and turned away. The Prophet 🕊 immediately comforted her and explained his initial statement by adding:

أَخْبِرُوهَا أَنَّهَا لَا تَدْخُلُهَا وَهِيَ عَجُوزٌ

"Let her know that she will not enter it as an old person."

He then recited the following verse to further stress his answer:

إِنَّا أَنْشَأْنَاهُنَّ إِنْشَاءً فَجَعَلْنَاهُنَّ أَبْكَارًا عُرُبًا أَتْرَابًا

"Indeed, We will have perfectly created their mates, making them virgins, loving and of equal age."[6]

Upon reading this set of verses, one may naturally ask: is this a reference to the believing women of Paradise or is it an allusion to the *ḥūr al-ʿīn*, who are the special maidens allotted to the male believers? The prevailing dispute on this question

---

6 *al-Wāqiʿah*, 35-37.

is in fact immaterial, since the fact of the matter is that any dimension of beauty that is allotted to the *ḥūr al-ʿīn* applies to the believing women *a fortiori*. In fact, in one notable narration, the Mother of the Believers Umm Salamah ﵂ posed the following query to the Prophet ﷺ:

يَا رَسُولَ اللهِ: نِسَاءُ الدُّنْيَا أَفْضَلُ أم الحُورُ العِينُ

"O Messenger of Allah, are the believing women of this world better or the ḥūr al-ʿīn?"

The Prophet ﷺ beautifully answered her question by using a marvellous simile:

بَلْ نِسَاءُ الدُّنْيَا أَفْضَلُ مِنَ الحُورِ العِيْنِ، كَفَضْلِ الظهَارَةِ عَلَى البطانةِ

"Rather, the women of this world are better than the ḥūr al-ʿīn just as the outer lining of the garment is more beautiful than its inner lining."

This response evoked the surprise of Umm Salamah ﵂, who further enquired:

وَبِمَ ذَاكَ يَا رَسُول اللهِ؟

"And on what basis is that, O Messenger of Allah?"

The Prophet ﷺ clarified by stating:

بِصَلاَتِهِنَّ وَصِيَامِهِنَّ وَعِبَادَتِهِنَّ

"This is the case owing to their ṣalāh (prayer), ṣiyām, and others acts of ʿibādah."

From this narration, we may deduce that upon entering Paradise, the believing women will not only be allotted an unprecedented degree of physical beauty, they will also be further adorned and beautified as a result of the light from their persistent acts of *'ibādah*. Their beauty will be so breathtaking and astonishing that the noble Companion Ibn 'Abbās ☙ said: "If a woman of Paradise were to display their wrist between the Heavens and the Earth, the entirety of creation would be dazzled by her beauty. If she happened to display her veil or her garment, they would eclipse the light of the Sun. And if she were to reveal her face, its beauty would illuminate every existing thing that is found between the Heavens and the Earth." As such, the beauty of the female believer will be so intense that the normal dimensions of the temporal world would not be capable of absorbing its light and splendour. Not only will the form of our bodies be fundamentally different, the functions of our limbs will vary as well. In an authentic Hadith, the Prophet ﷺ said: "The people of Paradise will eat and drink, but they will not blow their noses, nor will they need to relieve themselves, digest their food, or urinate." Thus, unlike in the case of this temporal world, humans will not face any complications or forms of discomfort that are associated with urination, defecation, and menstruation.

Yet, this fact leads to an obvious problem: if the believers will be continuously consuming exquisite foods and drinking fine wines during their eternal stay in Paradise, will they not in some way or form need to digest and excrete these edibles in some way or form? In response to this question, one must appreciate the fact that in Paradise, there are no limits to what is possible, which ultimately implies that a different mechanism exists. In one report, the Prophet ﷺ said that the means of excretion in Paradise would consist of sweating and burping musk. Neither of the two will occur due to discomfort or indigestion, but instead they will spur the believers to glorify Allah with full happiness and pleasure. In this world, Muslims usually say *alḥamdulillāh* after they sneeze, but in the Hereafter, they will be reciting it in a more natural and fluid manner. After evaluating the myriad of reports that are found in this matter, there are a number of scholars who argue that humanity was decreed to live on this Earth as a temporary layover to relieve themselves and excrete the forbidden fruit that was consumed by our first parents, Adam ﷺ and Ḥawwā' ﷺ. If this interpretation is accepted, then it ultimately implies that our time in this temporal world is nothing more than a brief stop to excrete the physical and spiritual waste that is found in our bodies. Taking these facts into account, other questions naturally arise. For instance, once situated in Paradise, will the bodies of the believers possess organs? On this question, Muslim theologians have tendered a number of responses. Some of them reached the conclusion that the believers will have an entirely different bodily structure with no organs being present. Others argued that whilst the believers will continue to possess organs in the Afterlife, their constitution and function will be entirely different from that in this world. To illustrate this point, one may consider a number of Hadiths which suggest that the believers will be transparent or translucent beings. In one Hadith, the Prophet ﷺ mentioned that within the blissful plane of Paradise, the bone marrow of the female believer will be observable. Due to our limited knowledge, we may not be able to appreciate the full import of this report and the beauty being alluded to here, but it will become fully comprehensible in the Hereafter.

With regard to communication, there is the question of what language the believers will be conversing in during their permanent stay in Paradise. In this matter, there are a number of narrations which indicate that the people of Jannah will converse with one another in the Arabic language. However, the scholars of Hadith have deemed these reports to be inauthentic. Another group of commentators argue that these reports collectively have sufficient strength and constitute evidence in the matter. They also add that it is possible for Allah to grant all the believers the natural capacity to converse in the language without any difficulty. Regardless of which side has struck the mark, there can be no doubt that the believers will have a collective means of communication between them.

Upon evaluating these various reports, one must appreciate the fact that they will not obtain the beautiful bodily form of Paradise if they fail to properly maintain their worldly bodies towards the path of Allah and the service of His religion.

On the Day of Judgement, every person will be asked how they used their body in this life. To obtain the beautiful bodily form of Paradise, believers must aim to maintain their worldly bodies towards the path of Allah and the service of His religion in this world.

This is why during the main trial of the Day of Judgement one of the main questions that every person will be asked is the following:

عَنْ جَسَدِهِ فِيمَا أَبْلاهُ

"...[and he will be asked] about his body, that is, concerning how he used it."

This connection between the worldly body and its form in the Hereafter is perhaps pronounced most greatly in the case of the *shuhadā'* (martyrs), as illustrated in a Hadith which states: "As they once did with blood, the wounds of the *shuhadā'* will be flowing with beauty on the Day of Judgement." Instead of being stained with pungent smell that is traditionally found with blood, the wounds of the martyrs will emit the pleasant fragrance of pure musk, which will be superior to any form of perfume found in this world.

As Muslims, we must always aim to perform actions and deeds that will amplify our bodily constitution in the Hereafter. One key course of action that can be undertaken to achieve this end is improving our character. After all, in the Arabic language, there is a linguistic connection between the words *khuluq* (character) and *khalq* (bodily state). This explains why the Prophet ﷺ used to constantly supplicate:

اللَّهُمَّ كَمَا أَحْسَنْتَ خَلْقِي فَأَحْسِنْ خُلُقِي

"O Allah, just as You have beautified my outer bodily state, beautify my inner state as well."

Thus, in order to have your physical form beautified in Jannah, it is imperative that you adopt a beautiful mode of comportment in this worldly life. If you concentrate on amplifying your inner state in this world, Allah ﷻ will reciprocate by amplifying your beauty in the other world.

ادْخُلُوهَا بِسَلَامٍ آمِنِينَ

(It will be said to the believers)

"Enter (Jannah) in peace and security."

AL-ḤIJR, 46

4

Your Heavenly Welcome

The noble Companion ʿAlī ibn Abī Ṭālib ﷺ is reported to have said: "Those who are mindful of their Lord will be led to the Garden. Once they arrive at its gate, they will come across a tree; at the base of that tree there will be two flowing streams. After being commanded to do so, they will approach one of them and drink from it. As a result, all the filth and foulness within them will be washed away. They will then proceed to drink from the other stream and make *wuḍū'* from its water, which will cause all their outer filth to be washed away. This process will ultimately confer them a Jannah-like radiance." To add to this awesome and breathtaking account, ʿAlī followed his statement by providing the following description of the believers in Paradise: "Their skin will never change and never crack. Their hair will never become dishevelled, and it will appear as if it had been polished. After obtaining this state, they will reach the Keepers of Paradise, who will say to them:

سَلَٰمٌ عَلَيْكُمْ طِبْتُمْ فَٱدْخُلُوهَا خَٰلِدِينَ

"[The Angels of Paradise will say:] 'Peace be upon you! You have done well, so come in, to stay forever.'"[7]

The same message of peace was expressed by the blessed Prophet ﷺ when he migrated to the city of Medina and addressed its inhabitants for the first time. When he proceeded to enumerate the various means to obtaining Paradise, he first mentioned the following factor:

أَفْشُوا السَّلَام

"Spread the salām (greeting of peace) to others."

The final statement that is expressed in this beautiful Hadith reiterates this same sentiment:

تَدْخُلُو الجَنَّةَ بِالسَّلَام

"[If you do the aforementioned ordinances] you will enter Jannah in peace."

Thus, if you wish to receive the greeting of *salām* from the Angels in Paradise, then it is imperative that you become an

---

[7] *Zumar*, 73.

In Paradise, a person will be dressed with special garments, adorned with jewellery, and will be shown palaces of gold and silver. The intensity of pleasure will not diminish, as the believer will continue to experience the level of happiness that they sensed when they first entered.

ambassador of peace in this temporal world. To appreciate this point, the greeting of the Angels—which was cited above—requires an additional layer of analysis. In their declaration, the Angels first state: "*Salām 'alaykum* (Peace be upon you)." This is an indication that the believer will be submerged in peace and safeguarded from any form of danger or harm. Thereafter, the Angels address the believers by stating, "*Ṭibtum*". This can be translated to read, "You have done well", or "You have become purified". Such an expression reflects the pure internal disposition of the believers and the fact that they are secure from the effects of any of their past sins. Then the Angels will say: "*Fadkhulūhā khālidīn* (So come in, to stay forever)." This beautiful closing statement is not to be read as an imperative, but instead it reflects a solemn promise to the believers that they will remain in Paradise forever and without any deterioration of their state. In other words, not only will they be protected from any removal or expulsion, they will also be immune from the conventional vicissitudes found in the worldly plane, such as aging, death, or attacks from external enemies. In stark contrast, the disbelievers will be subject to a myriad of humiliating questions and cross-examinations on the part of the Angels, with the former being reminded that they were provided a myriad of signs from the Prophets and Messengers ﷺ. These taunts and provocations will only further intensify the pain of the disbelievers, since their hearts will be filled with regret and sorrow due to their failure to follow the true message of Islam. But their affair will only worsen after they are ordered to enter the Hellfire in the worst state of humiliation. Allah ﷻ and His Angels will address them by stating:

ٱدْخُلُوٓا۟ أَبْوَٰبَ جَهَنَّمَ

"[It will be said to them:] 'Enter the gates of Hell, to stay there forever.'"[8]

There is a subtle yet important difference found between this call made to the disbelievers and the address made to the believers:

ادْخُلُوهَا

"...so come in..."[9]

After looking at these two verses, one deduces that the disbelievers will be required to pass a number of gates before being submerged in the Fire. The added step of going through these gates will only add to their pain and humiliation, since whenever they pass one, it will be shut and thus increase their feeling of discomfort and isolation. The added layer of humiliation and tribulation that arises due to these sealed gates is chillingly described in the following set of verses:

إِنَّهَا عَلَيْهِم مُّؤْصَدَةٌ فِى عَمَدٍ مُّمَدَّدَةٍ

"It [the Fire] will be sealed over them, tightly secured with long braces."[10]

---

8 *Zumar*, 72.

9 *Zumar*, 73.

10 *Humazah*, 8-9.

According to the Qur'anic commentators, these braces and columns will seal the gates of Hell just as a giant stone keeps a door secure. In contrast, the people of Paradise will be told:

ادْخُلُوهَا بِسَلَامٍ آمِنِينَ

"[It will be said to them,] 'Enter in peace and security.'"[11]

The believers will be told to enter the eternal abode of bliss in peace, since in logical terms a person who has attained salvation will never wish to exit such a euphoric plane. And since no person would wish to leave this blessed Garden, it follows that no gates or doors will be needed for the purposes of enclosing the inhabitants or preventing their departure. This explains why the verse addressing the believers orders them to directly enter Paradise, since there will be no doors interposing between them and their final destination. Moreover, a person who is appointed a spot in Paradise will not need a guide or aide, since they will be provided the divine inspiration to find their residence. In fact, in a beautiful Hadith the Prophet ﷺ is reported to have said:

فَوَالَّذِي نَفْسُ مُحَمَّدٍ بِيَدِهِ لَأَحَدُهُمْ بِمَسْكَنِهِ فِي الْجَنَّةِ أَدَلُّ بِمَنْزِلِهِ كَانَ فِي الدُّنْيَا

"By the One in Whose Hand is Muhammad's soul, every one of you will know their dwelling place in Paradise better or as much as they knew their residence in this world."

[11] *Ḥijr*, 46.

This beautiful Hadith constitutes as a vivid explanation of the following Qur'anic verse:

وَيُدۡخِلُهُمُ ٱلۡجَنَّةَ عَرَّفَهَا لَهُمۡ

"...and [He will] admit them into Paradise, having made it known to them."[12]

Regarding this verse, the noble Successor al-Ḥasan al-Baṣrī ﷺ is reported to have said:

وَصَفَ اللهُ تَعَالَى لَهُمُ الجَنَّةَ فِي الدُّنْيَا فَلَمَّا دَخَلُوهَا عَرَفُوهَا بِصِفَتِهِ

"Allah has described Paradise to them in this world in such a manner that once they enter it, they will know it by virtue of its description."

Thus, every Muslim will already be well-acquainted with the description of Jannah, whereby they will possess the ability to navigate the eternal plane of happiness and find their designated castle. Thus, the Angel that accompanies the believer to their appointed spot in Paradise does not constitute a guide, but instead functions as a wisher of glad tidings. The famous Qur'anic commentator Muqātil ibn Ḥayyān ﷺ provided further details concerning the role of this companion Angel by stating: "We have been informed that the Angel entrusted with the care of the children of Adam will walk in Paradise. The child of Adam will follow him, and he will present to him all his properties until he

12 *Muhammad*, 6.

reaches his final dwelling." As such, the role of the Angel is restricted to presenting the believer their allotted place in Paradise as well as their belongings and possessions. Once the believer enters their residence and is accompanied by their family members, the Angel will depart. According to some narrations, before turning away, the Angel will address the believer by stating:

أَنَا قَيِّمُكَ الذِي وُكِلْتُ بِأَمْرِك

"I am your caretaker and have been entrusted to you."

In another important account, the famous Successor Ḥumayd ibn Hilāl 🕮 is reported to have said: "When a person enters Paradise, is provided the form of the people of Paradise, dressed with the garments of the people of Paradise, adorned with their jewellery, and is shown the maidens, servants, and the other beings of Paradise, they will become so pleased that if it was possible, they would die out of joy. It will then be said to this person: 'Do you notice this degree of happiness that is overwhelming you? It will last like this forever!'" In other words, the intensity of pleasure will always remain in the same degree, as the believer will continue to experience the level of happiness that they sensed when they first entered Paradise. Similarly, it is reported that al-Ḍaḥḥāk 🕮 said: "When the believer proceeds and enters Jannah, the Angel will lead him to all of its different lanes and pathways and say: 'What do you see here?' Then one will say: 'I see palaces of gold and silver.' In response, the Angel will say: 'All of that is for you.'

Once he reaches that site, there will be servants at the gate of every palace who will welcome him and say:

نَحْنُ لَك

'We are for you.'

Then the Angel will say: 'Walk further with me.' Once they advance, he will then say: 'What do you see here?' The person will say: 'I see beautiful canopies and companions.' It will then be said to him: 'All of this is for you.' Then one will reach there and will be received by them, with all of them saying:

نَحْنُ لَك

'We are for you.'"

Another astounding report concerning the wonders of Paradise is related by an early forerunner of the Muslim ummah, namely Abū 'Abd al-Raḥmān al-Jubarī ﵀, who states: "When the believer first enters Paradise, he will be received by 70,000 servants who will bear the appearance of glimmering pearls. Two rows of those servants will be arranged on both sides, with neither one of them seeing the other. At any moment he walks, they will follow him and walk with him. And the spouses of Paradise will welcome one another by saying:

أَنْتَ حِبِّي وَأنَا حِبُّك

'You are my love and I am your love.'"

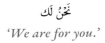

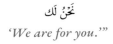

But on that fateful day, the greatest welcomer of all will undoubtedly be none other than Allah Himself. In an authentic Hadith, the Prophet ﷺ said that Allah ﷻ will address the people of Paradise by saying:

يَا أَهْلَ الجَنَّة

"O people of Paradise!"

The inhabitants of Paradise will respond to their Lord's call by stating:

لَبَّيْكَ وَسَعَدَيْكَ

"Here we are, O Lord, willingly and seeking Your pleasure."

This response reflects their earnest desire to please their Creator and immediately comply with His demands. Throughout their life in this temporal world, the believers sought the pleasure of their Lord, and now even in Paradise, they are eager to respond to Allah's commands. After receiving their positive response, Allah ﷻ will say:

هَل رَضِيتُم

"Are you pleased?"

The believers will be stunned by this question. They will address their Creator and ask: "How could we not be pleased when You have given us everything that we could possibly desire and have allotted things that You have not given to any other member of Your creation?" But in response, Allah ﷻ will say: "I will in fact give you something that is better than all of that." The believers will ask: "Our Lord, and what can be better than that?" Allah ﷻ will then state:

أُحِلُّ عليكُم رِضْوانِي، فلا أَسْخَطُ عليكُم بَعْدَهُ أَبَدًا

"I will be pleased with you forever and I will never be angry with you again."

This remarkable tradition reflects the unlimited breadth of Allah's pleasure. Had He never been initially pleased with the believers, He would not have blessed them with the bounties and beauties of Paradise. But in this address, He provides the believers the greatest conceivable blessing: His perpetual contentedness. This declaration will only further amplify the happiness of the believers.

The houses of the believers will be elaborately designed and structured, and will vary depending on the specific deeds and qualities of the believers. The distinguished friends of Allah ﷻ will be allotted special homes due to their persistence upon the faith and their marvellous ability to overcome major worldly trials with unwavering patience. In sum, these special champions of the faith are individuals who sought the pleasure of Allah at all costs, regardless of

In Paradise, a person will identify their place and be joined by their family members who will receive them with joy. When they observe all their blessings and pleasures, they will recite: "Praise be to Allah for guiding us to this. We would have never been guided if Allah had not guided us."

the challenges and afflictions they had to undergo. An example of such a distinguished figure is Āsiyah 🌸, who prayed to Allah 🌼 and said:

رَبِّ ٱبْنِ لِي عِندَكَ بَيْتًا فِي ٱلْجَنَّةِ

"My Lord! Build me a house in Paradise near You." [13]

What is remarkable about Āsiyah's prayer is that she made this supplication to Allah whilst she was being tormented in this world and was deprived of the most basic of comforts. But she accepted these sacrifices all for the sake of her Lord. Likewise, there is a beautiful narration where Allah 🌼 issued His *salām* (greeting of peace) to Khadījah 🌸 and communicated to her the *bushrā* (glad tiding) of a pearl-encrusted palace in Jannah, wherein she will live in eternally in a state of peace and tranquility. This is in light of the fact that she made many sacrifices in this worldly life to support the Prophet 🌼 and assist him in the propagation of the Islamic call. Moreover, in an authentic narration, the Prophet 🌼 said that if a person loses a child but exercises patience by praising Allah, Allah will construct a house for him in Paradise in light of the fact that they lost their loved one in this world.

To close this chapter, it would be befitting to cite a spectacular statement made by Ibn Qayyim al-Jawziyyah 🌸. After first asking us to imagine our place in Paradise, he says: "A person will enter into Paradise and identify their place. Thereafter, they

---

13 *al-Taḥrīm*, 11.

will be joined by their family members, who will receive them with joy, especially if this union occurs after a particular loved one had departed for a relatively long period. Then he will hear the greetings of all the new companions of Paradise. As he proceeds to recline on his bed and evaluates its foundation, he will find that the bed has been erected on beautiful pearls. His gaze will then fall on the green, red, and yellow paths and drapes that lay before him. Then he will raise his head and observe the roof of his house; had he not been created for it, he would have lost his vision."

Ibn al-Qayyim ﷺ closes his statement by noting that when the believer observes the blessings and pleasures that have been conferred on him in Paradise, he will recite the following verse:

ٱلْحَمْدُ لِلَّهِ ٱلَّذِى هَدَىٰنَا لِهَٰذَا وَمَا كُنَّا لِنَهْتَدِىَ لَوْلَآ أَنْ هَدَىٰنَا ٱللَّهُ

"Praise be to Allah for guiding us to this. We would have never been guided if Allah had not guided us."[14]

[14] *al-A'rāf*, 43.

5

Your Home in Jannah

After being granted one's residence in Jannah and being welcomed by Allah, the Angels, and the rest of the believers, the natural question is how one's permanent stay in Paradise will be. In this regard, Abū Hurayrah reported that both he and some other Companions once said to the Prophet ﷺ: "O Messenger of Allah, when we see you, our hearts become softened and we feel as if we are from the people of the Hereafter. But then after we depart and leave you, we become immersed in the affairs of the *dunyā* (temporal world), become preoccupied with our spouses and children, and ultimately find our hearts to be hardened." The Prophet ﷺ alleviated their concerns by stating: "If you were to remain upon the same state that you are in when with me, the Angels would shake hands with you and visit you in your homes. And if you were to not commit sins, Allah would replace you with another group of people who will commit sins, such that they will seek His forgiveness and He will forgive them."

This report serves as an acute reminder that perfection is unachievable in the temporary worldly life. Such a state is only achievable in Paradise; it is due to this moral excellence that the Angels will come and visit a person during every moment that they find themselves in the permanent abode of bliss. During our stayover in this world, our goal should be to emulate this moral standard as much as possible, so that we may actualise that excellence and perfection in the permanent realm. After being relieved by the Prophet's words cited above, the Companions ﷺ proceeded to ask the Prophet ﷺ: "O Messenger of Allah, tell us about Jannah and its structure." The Prophet ﷺ then said:

لَبِنَةٌ مِّن فِضَّةٌ وَلَبِنَةٌ مِّن ذَهَبٌ وَمِلَاطُهَا الْمِسْكُ الْأَذْفَرُ وَحَصْبَؤُهَا اللُّؤْلُ
وَالْيَاقُوتُ وَتُرْبَتُهَا الزَّعْفَرَانُ

"Its structure is one brick of gold and one brick of silver. Its plaster is musk, its gravel consists of pearls and rubies, and its soil comprises of saffron."

After providing this awe-inspiring description of the structure of Paradise, the Prophet ﷺ said:

مَنْ دَخَلَهَا يَنْعَمُ وَلَا يَبْأَسُ وَيَخْلُدُ وَلَا يَمُوتُ، لَا تَبْلَى ثِيَابُهُمْ وَلَا يَفْنَى شَبَابُهُمْ

"Whoever enters it will always be prosperous and will never grieve and will enjoy a life of eternity that precludes death. Their clothes will never fade, and their young comely state shall never expire."

In the last chapter, a golden quotation from Imam Ibn Qayyim al-Jawziyyah ﷺ was cited concerning the dimensions of the houses of Paradise. After examining reports and narrations related in the matter, Ibn al-Qayyim ﷺ deduced that the residences of the people of Paradise will have a height of approximately 100 cubits. Moreover, these towering structures will be adjacent to colourful waterfalls that possess pearls and rubies. Water will hence be flowing in near proximity to one's dwelling, which will yield a beautiful sight. But one will not have a single or a few houses in Paradise; instead, they will have a myriad of houses. For Allah ﷻ says:

وَمَسَاكِنَ طَيِّبَةً فِي جَنَّاتِ عَدْنٍ

"... [they will have] splendid homes in the Gardens of Eternity..."[15]

15 *al-Tawbah*, 72.

One notices that in this verse the word *masākin* is used, which is the plural form for *maskan* (home). Thus, not only will a person possess several mansions, every one of these units will be fully-furnished and complete, with no form of renovations, furniture, or utilities needed. What makes the prospects of the believer even greater is that he will be granted a variety of properties. This explains why the existing Islamic texts use a number of different labels or terms for denoting the various properties that the believer will possess in Paradise. These include the following structures: *buyūt* (homes), *quṣūr* (palaces), *ghuraf* (special rooms), and *khiyām* (guest houses and pavilions). In light of these innumerable blessings and allotment of possessions, Allah ﷻ says:

وَإِذَا رَأَيْتَ ثَمَّ رَأَيْتَ نَعِيمًا وَمُلْكًا كَبِيرًا

"And if you looked around, you would see bliss and a vast kingdom."[16]

Such a sight will immensely please the believer and fill their heart with joy, for Allah states in the Qur'an:

تَعْرِفُ فِي وُجُوهِهِمْ نَضْرَةَ النَّعِيمِ

"You will recognise on their faces the glow of delight."[17]

16 *al-Insān*, 20.

17 *Muṭaffifīn*, 24.

The more the believer gazes around their surroundings, the more their happiness and state of bliss will grow as they see all the palaces and castles constructed solely in their name. The next question that naturally arises is whether there are any reports concerning the nature of these residences. There are in fact a plethora of Hadiths which provide answers in this regard. For instance, in a divinely-inspired night vision, the Prophet ﷺ observed a golden palace—whose quality was higher and purer than anything seen in this world—built for the noble Companion ʿUmar ibn al-Khaṭṭāb ؓ. The famous Successor al-Ḥasan al-Baṣrī ؒ commented on these reports by stating: "A palace of pure gold is only reserved for a Prophet, *ṣiddīq* (champion of the truth), martyr, and a just ruler." These classes are quite similar to the seven categories of people that will be provided shade under the Throne of Allah. Such a parallel is intuitive, since it would be logical for the eminent ranks bestowed on the Day of Judgement to be transferred into Paradise as well. Regarding the different types of palaces in Paradise, Ibn al-Qayyim ؒ states: "There are palaces in Paradise that are made of gold, silver, pearls, rubies, or crystals." In a similar manner, the Companion ʿUbayd ibn ʿUmayr ؓ is reported to have said: "The lowest person in Paradise will have a home of one single pearl alongside its myriad of rooms and gates."

In Paradise, the *ghuraf* will be the highest and most prominent of structures, and they will be exclusively reserved for the best of people, who are known as the *sābiqūn* (forerunners). In a Hadith, it is mentioned that the *ghuraf* are made of elegant crystals and they emit marvellous and awesome flashes of light throughout the horizon of Paradise. From the viewpoint of the lower-ranking members of Paradise, they will appear like brilliant chandeliers and stars. In one famous Hadith, the Prophet ﷺ is reported to have said: "The rest of the people of Jannah will see the quarters of these *ghuraf* just as you see a long-gone star in the horizon."

It is now worthwhile to explore the distinguishing qualities of the *sābiqūn* so that we may aspire to attain their rank and become possessors of the *ghuraf* in the Hereafter. In a number of Qur'anic verses, Allah ﷻ has highlighted a myriad of features and characteristics that the owners of the *ghuraf* possess. For instance, in one verse, He says:

لَٰكِنِ الَّذِينَ اتَّقَوْا رَبَّهُمْ لَهُمْ غُرَفٌ مِّن فَوْقِهَا غُرَفٌ مَّبْنِيَّةٌ تَجْرِي مِن تَحْتِهَا الْأَنْهَارُ

"But, for those who fear their Lord, there are chambers with chambers built on top of them, with rivers running from underneath them. This is Allah's promise. Allah does not go back on any promise."[18]

From this verse, one infers that a fundamental quality of the owners of the *ghuraf* is *taqwā* (God-consciousness), whereby a person exerts their best efforts to avoid falling into sin and to regulate their lower selves.

18 *Zumar*, 20.

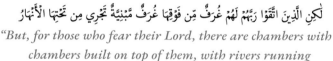

The more the believer will gaze around their surroundings in Paradise, the more their happiness and state of bliss will grow as they see all the palaces and castles constructed solely in their name.

Moreover, in another key verse pertinent to the same topic, Allah ﷻ states:

إِلَّا مَنْ ءَامَنَ وَعَمِلَ صَٰلِحًا فَأُو۟لَٰٓئِكَ لَهُمْ جَزَآءُ ٱلضِّعْفِ بِمَا عَمِلُوا۟ وَهُمْ فِى ٱلْغُرُفَٰتِ ءَامِنُونَ

"But those who believe and do good—it is they who will have a multiplied reward for what they did, and they will be secure in mansions."[19]

From this verse, one derives the fact that the consistent performance of good deeds is instrumental for attaining salvation in the Hereafter and possessing the exquisite *ghuraf*. Put another way, lofty deeds lead to lofty dwellings. In a marvellous tradition reported by the Companion Abū Mālik al-Ashʿarī ؓ, the Prophet ﷺ said: "There are rooms in Paradise where the inner portions are seen from the outside realm and the outside realm is seen from the inner portions." The existence of such prominent and transparent homes captivated the hearts of the Companions, who asked: "O Messenger of Allah, to whom do these rooms belong?" In response, the Prophet ﷺ said: "Allah has prepared them for the one who feeds the poor, fasts consistently, and prays during the night whilst others are sleeping."

Additional indicators and characteristics can be found in Sūrah al-Furqān, where Allah ﷻ provides a vivid description of the *ʿibād al-Raḥmān* (servants of the Most Merciful).

---

[19] *Saba'*, 37.

Amongst the key qualities that are mentioned concerning this special class of believers is that they trek on the Earth with humility and respond to mischief-makers and evildoers by issuing the *salām* (greeting of peace) and refusing to reciprocate. In other words, they exercise patience and contentment in the face of all the tribulations and trials found in the temporal world. These are the characteristics of the people who are loved by their Creator. As a result of their moral excellence in this world, Allah ﷻ will ensure that they are handsomely rewarded in the Hereafter:

أُوْلَٰٓئِكَ يُجْزَوْنَ ٱلْغُرْفَةَ بِمَا صَبَرُوا۟

"It is they who will be rewarded with mansions for their perseverance."[20]

Because they were paragons of virtue in the worldly life and responded to the evildoers with *salām*, Allah ﷻ will reciprocate in the Hereafter by issuing His own *salām*, which in essence requires a permanent life of peace and tranquility in the best of dwellings.

Another quality found in this superior class is their lack of interest in engaging in arguments with others, for the sake of maintaining the ties of brotherhood and friendship. The Prophet ﷺ mentioned that a home is promised for the one who avoids engaging in arguments with others, even if he is right. As such, the possessor of the *ghuraf* is an individual of

20 *al-Furqān*, 75.

impeccable character and a person who maintains a balanced temperament in their daily interactions; as such, they leave off any immoral modes of behaviour, such as crude humour, immodest exchanges, or the use of profanities. If a person wishes to have high-rise houses in the Hereafter, then they must adopt high standards in this world. The possession of a multiplicity of palaces and residences in Paradise is possible provided that we commit to performing a multiplicity of good deeds in this world.

ادْخُلُوهَا بِسَلَامٍ آمِنِينَ

(It will be said to the believers)

"Enter (Jannah) in peace and security."

AL-ḤIJR, 46

6

How to Build Homes in Jannah

The previous section of this work aimed to establish a number of fundamental points concerning the houses of Paradise. It confirmed that some mansions are conferred to a believer due to the *ṣabr* (patience) that they exercised in this world, as demonstrated in the shining examples of Āsiyah عليها السلام, Khadījah رضي الله عنها, and the *ʿibād al-Raḥmān*. Another category of mansions can be traced to the performance of pious deeds in the worldly life. The purpose of this chapter is to identify and classify these pious acts, which according to our scheme number 10 in total.

The first five of these deeds fall under the domain of *'ibādah* (acts of worship). The most important of these actions consists of playing a role in the construction of a *masjid* for the sake of Allah. In this regard, the Prophet ﷺ has said in a mass-transmitted report: "Whoever builds a *masjid* for Allah, Allah will build for them a home in Paradise." This is an incredible form of reciprocation from the Lord of all worlds which is purely in the interest of the Muslim. A Muslim builds a house for Allah's sake despite His kingdom being boundless and free of any shortcoming, whilst in the Hereafter Allah ﷻ commissions the construction of a palace for this Muslim, despite the latter having no domain or sphere of influence. Whilst it is true that it is very difficult for a single person to fund the construction of a given *masjid*, it should be noted that even funding the smallest portion of a Muslim place of worship can yield immense dividends in the Hereafter.

The second golden act of worship that is established in the Prophetic Sunnah is performing the 12 voluntary *rak'ahs* (units) of prayer on a daily basis within one's dwelling. Not only was this the practice of the Prophet ﷺ himself, he also urged his followers to emulate this standard as well by stating: "Whoever prays 12 *rak'ahs* besides the obligatory prayers for the sake of Allah, Allah will build a home in Paradise for them." The 12 *rak'ahs* of prayer that are being referred to in this Hadith consist of the following: two before Fajr, four before Ẓuhr, two after Ẓuhr, two after Maghrib, and two after 'Ishā'. Unfortunately, it is common to find that many Muslims restrict themselves to exclusively performing the obligatory prayers out of the pretext that they will be deprived of their work productivity, a factor which will negatively affect their monthly earnings. However, a Muslim should think strategically and appreciate the fact that no salary in this world can equal the blessing of having a mansion in Paradise. It is also important to note that the performance of these additional voluntary prayers only requires approximately 15–20 minutes of one's time per day. In fact, the time required could be even less if we take into account another Hadith which states: "Whoever prays the four *rak'ahs* of *ishrāq* (sunrise) and then follows it with four *rak'ahs* before the Ẓuhr prayer, Allah will build a house for him in Paradise."

The next praiseworthy quality is extremely easy and can be performed in a matter of minutes during any part of the day. In a powerful Hadith, the Prophet ﷺ said:

مَنْ قَرَأَ: قُلْ هُوَ اللّٰهُ أَحَدٌ عِشْرِينَ مَرَّةً بَنَى اللّٰهُ لَهُ قَصْرًا فِي الجَنَّةِ

"Whoever reads Qul Huwa Allāhu Aḥad (i.e., Sūrah al-Ikhlāṣ) twenty times, Allah will build for them a castle in Paradise."

The immense virtue found in this short chapter lies in the fact that it constitutes the key to Paradise, for it eloquently encapsulates the *kalimah al-ikhlāṣ* (statement of sincerity) embedded within the declaration of *lā ilāha illa Allāh* (there is no God but Allah). If a person reads the chapter more than the outlined number, then with the permission of Allah, they will have several houses in Paradise that are registered in their name.

Another way to obtain a house in Paradise is to persistently make a special *du'ā'* (supplication) before falling asleep. Before sleeping, the Prophet ﷺ advised the members of his ummah to perform *wuḍū'*, lie on the right side of their body, and recite:

اللَّهُمَّ أَسْلَمْتُ وجْهِي إِلَيْكَ، وفَوَّضْتُ أَمْرِي إِلَيْكَ، وأَلْجَأْتُ ظَهْرِي إِلَيْكَ، رَغْبَةً ورَهْبَةً إِلَيْكَ، لَا مَلْجَأَ ولَا مَنْجَا مِنْكَ إِلَّا إِلَيْكَ، اللَّهُمَّ آمَنْتُ بِكِتَابِكَ الَّذِي أَنْزَلْتَ، وبِنَبِيِّكَ الذي أَرْسَلْتَ

"O Allah, I submit myself to You. I entrust my affairs to You. I turn my face to You and I lay myself depending upon You, having hope in You whilst also fearing You. There is no refuge and no escape from You except to You. O Allah, I believe in Your Book (i.e., the Qur'an) that You revealed, and the Prophet that You sent."

In one version of this narration, the Prophet ﷺ said that the one who recites this supplication before sleeping and happens to die on that night will depart this life upon the *fiṭrah* (natural disposition). In another version, he stated that a home will be built in Paradise in this person's name. The beauty of this reward lies in the fact that Allah positively responds to the believer's request for shelter and refuge by providing him a palace that will provide him eternal happiness in Paradise.

The fifth and last form of devotional act of worship is a special formula of *dhikr* (remembrance of the divine) that one makes when they enter the marketplace, regardless of whether the shopping centre in question is physical or virtual in nature. As such, even if someone is purchasing a product online, it is recommended for them to make this supplication. This supplication is established in a magnificent Hadith of the Prophet ﷺ, who is reported to have said:

مَنْ قَالَ فِي السُّوقِ: لَا إِلَهَ إِلَّا اللهُ وَحْدَهُ لَا شَرِيكَ لَهُ لَهُ الْمُلْكُ وَلَهُ الْحَمْدُ يُحْيِي وَيُمِيتُ وَهُوَ حَيٌّ لَا يَمُوتُ، بِيَدِهِ الْخَيْرُ وَهُوَ عَلَى كُلِّ شَيْءٍ قَدِيرٌ، كَتَبَ اللهُ لَهُ أَلْفَ أَلْفِ حَسَنَةٍ وَمَحَا عَنْهُ أَلْفَ أَلْفِ سَيِّئَةٍ وَبَنَى لَهُ بَيْتًا فِي الْجَنَّةِ

"If one is in the marketplace and recites, 'None has the right to be worshipped except Allah alone, He has no partner, to Him belongs all sovereignty and praise, He gives life and causes death, He is ever living and does not die, in His Hand is all good and He has power over all things', Allah will register for him a million good deeds, wipe away a million sins from his record, and build a house for him in Paradise."

This Hadith reflects the infinite generosity of Allah ﷻ, for He rewards His servants if they happen to remember Him during their financial affairs and transactions. To ensure the acquisition of these immense rewards, one should never forget to recite this supplication whenever they enter the marketplace. The supplication made at the marketplace marks the conclusion of the first five means of having a house built in Paradise. These five factors consist of various acts of worship, such as calling to Allah ﷻ, remembering Him, praying to Him, and reciting His divine word.

The next cluster of deeds entails a fundamental metamorphosis in one's character through the improvement of interpersonal interactions and acts of worship. The importance of this set of deeds can be appreciated by considering the lofty rank of the *'ibād al-Raḥmān*, who are praised in the Qur'an for their exemplary character and their sole dependance on Allah ﷻ. Due to their intensely strong state of *tawakkul* (reliance on Allah), they are able to become paragons of patience and surmount any difficulties in this world. This is why Allah promises them the best of lodgings in the Hereafter:

أُوْلَٰٓئِكَ يُجْزَوْنَ ٱلْغُرْفَةَ بِمَا صَبَرُواْ

"It is they who will be rewarded with mansions for their perseverance."[21]

At this point, a person may naturally ask: what deeds should I perform on a regular basis in order to attain the rank of the *'ibād al-Raḥmān*? The answer to this question can be found in the remarkable Hadith narrated by the Companion Abū Mālik al-Ash'arī ﷺ, which was cited in the previous chapter. In that Hadith, the key distinguishing features of the *'ibād al-Raḥmān* were highlighted, namely their financial support for the poor and needy, observance of fasting during the day, and performance of the night prayer whilst the common folk

[21] *al-Furqān*, 75.

The Prophet ﷺ declared: "The closest to me in Jannah are the people with the best character." The person who leads a life of excellent character will have a house built in their name in Paradise, and their neighbour will be the best creation of Allah.

are asleep. But if the Qur'anic verses and Prophetic Hadiths concerning the elite servants of Allah are assessed more carefully, it will become evident that their key distinguishing qualities pertain to the heart and mind.

The first positive moral quality that the elite servants of Allah ﷻ consistently exercise and uphold in their daily interactions is *shukr* (gratitude). Such a powerful internal disposition bears a positive effect on their statements and actions, such as ensuring the financial needs of the poor are met. Only the people of *shukr* are able to fully abide by the ordinances outlined in the following Hadith:

أَفْشُوا السَّلَامَ وَأَطْعِمُوا الطَّعَام

"Spread the salām (greeting of peace) and feed the people."

The second positive deed that the Hadith of Abū Mālik al-Ash'arī ﷺ outlines is fasting, which is the highest demonstration of *ṣabr* (patience). In recognition of this unwavering perseverance and adoption of a frugal lifestyle, Allah will reward these believers handsomely by conferring them massive mansions in the highest points of Paradise. In one Hadith, the Prophet ﷺ is reported to have said: "A special gate is erected in Paradise for those who fast, and a distance spanning a journey of 70 years is placed between you and the Hellfire for every day that you fast." In logical terms, the more distant that one is from the Hellfire, the higher of a rank they will obtain in Paradise.

The final virtuous hallmark of the sincere believers is their continuous observance of the *tahajjud* prayer, which is done during the late night hours. In a sense, *tahajjud* prayer can be deemed a literal gateway to Paradise, as only the sincere servants of Allah would be willing to wake up every night and beseech their Lord. Because this practice is undertaken within the private confines of one's quarters, it is considered to be a perfect manifestation of *iḥsān* (religious excellence), which represents the epitome of Islamic character.

Another pristine quality which can be added to the above list of beautiful traits is *ḥilm* (forbearance), whereby a person exercises the utmost degree of caution and restraint in their daily interactions. This virtue is perhaps best exemplified when a person avoids engaging in arguments or debates with others in order to maintain the social bonds of the community. For this reason, the Prophet ﷺ said: "I guarantee a home on the outskirts of Paradise for the one who avoids argumentation, even when they are right." The party that unilaterally opts to withdraw from such discourses may be on the right, but wishes to avoid sparking a dispute for the greater good. In light of their patience and restraint, this elite class of the believers will be rewarded with beautiful houses in the peripheral regions of Paradise. Moreover, the Prophet ﷺ said he would guarantee a home in the centre of Paradise for the one who avoids lying, even whilst joking. This latter declaration highlights the centrality of the quality of *wara'* (caution), whereby a person avoids uttering any form of speech that may be of an inaccurate or deceitful nature.

A person who utters lies or words of deception risks compromising their standing in the Hereafter and their prospects for entering into Paradise. For this reason, the Prophet ﷺ said: "Truthfulness leads to Paradise." As such, if a Muslim ensures that their speech is truthful regardless of the existing trials or circumstances, they will be granted a place in Paradise.

These aforementioned qualities should not be seen in an isolated or broken fashion, since they are interrelated and link together to form of a cohesive whole known as *ḥusn al-khuluq* (excellent character). Thus, a person should aim to internalise all the previous qualities and exercise them on a daily basis. In this regard, the Prophet ﷺ said: "And I guarantee a home in the highest part of Paradise for the one who excels in character." In order to achieve this positive upshot, a person must formulate a firm and sincere intention to improve their character; in return, Allah will inculcate the aforementioned qualities within their disposition. Our blessed Prophet ﷺ, who possessed the best character amongst all of humankind, once declared: "The closest to me in Jannah are the people with the best character." As such, the person who leads a life of excellent character will not only have a house built in their name in Paradise, their neighbour in the blessed abode of bliss will be the best creation of Allah.

7

The Fragrance of Jannah

The believers who enter Paradise will find themselves in a permanent state of joy with their new bodily forms and their magnificent palaces. Such an environment will undoubtedly be breathtaking and overwhelming. One of the most pleasant aspects of Paradise will be its pleasant and gratifying fragrance, a factor which has been highlighted in several verses of the Qur'an and numerous Hadiths of the Prophet ﷺ. This is a thought-provoking fact, since it has been established by a number of studies that the sense of smell bears a stronger effect on the mind's impressions than taste.

The causal mechanism which accounts for this fact is that the sense of smell not only evokes memories from the past, but it also animates the mind concerning prospective future events. In this regard, a number of examples can be cited. For instance, after numerous years of bitter separation, the noble Prophet Yaʿqūb ﷺ was animated and invigorated after he smelled the garment of Prophet Yūsuf ﷺ, since it was an indication that his son was alive and in close proximity. Likewise, during the climax of the Battle of Uḥud, the noble Companion Anas ibn Naḍr ﷺ—who was the uncle of the famous Companion Anas ibn Mālik ﷺ—charged toward the enemy line of the Meccan polytheists when the rest of the Muslim army had collapsed and fallen in disarray. Anas ibn Naḍr ﷺ explained his brave and exceptional advance by stating:

إِنِّي أَجِدُ رِيحَ الْجَنَّةِ دُونَ أُحُدٍ

"I can smell the fragrance of Jannah behind Mount Uḥud."

With this declaration, Anas ibn Naḍr ﷺ was indicating that he could sense the proximity of Jannah in metaphysical terms, and he was so overjoyed with this divine grace that he immediately craved martyrdom in order to enter the abode of bliss. The fragrance of Paradise served as an acute reminder that the life of this lowly temporal world is of no value.

The sense of smell is also activated when the believer's soul is taken, since they are welcomed by the Angels with a pleasant fragrance, which serves as an early spectacle for the delights of Jannah that await them. The Prophet ﷺ is reported to have said regarding the death of the believers:

بَعَثَ اللهُ عَلَيْهِمْ رِيحًا طَيِّبًا

"Allah will send upon them gentle and pleasant breezes."

As such, the soul of the believer will depart from this world in a relaxed and tranquil state, for this fragrance will serve as a pleasant reminder of the domain that lies before them. This points to how strong and extensive the fragrance of Paradise is, for it will be realised and sensed outside of its defined parameters. In fact, there are some reports which confirm that the believers will be able to enjoy the fragrance of Paradise even before they enter it. For instance, in the well-known Hadith concerning the last person to enter Paradise, the Prophet ﷺ mentioned that the individual in question will be able to sense the fragrance of the Eternal Garden whilst standing outside its gates; such a perception will cause them to increase their longing for the permanent abode of bliss. In another Hadith, the Prophet ﷺ said: "Whoever kills a *dhimmī* (non-Muslim subject under the protection of Islamic rule), will not smell Paradise, even though its fragrance reaches a distance that exceeds even a hundred years." This report is remarkable in its import, since it provides insights concerning the far-reaching fragrance of Jannah by making reference to the dimensions and units of this world.

In a parallel fashion, during the miraculous night journey of al-Isrāʾ wa al-Miʿrāj, the Prophet ﷺ was taken aback by a strong and beautiful fragrance that was being emitted from one of the levels of Paradise. The Prophet ﷺ was surprised at the pleasant intensity of this sweet smell, so he turned to Jibrīl ﷺ and sought to identify its source. Jibrīl ﷺ accordingly responded: "It is the perfume of the hairdresser of the daughter of Fir'awn." The invocation of such a name may appear random at first, but this hairdresser was a young woman who secretly professed the true faith of monotheism. In terms of her professional role, she was tasked with the function of combing the hair of Fir'awn's daughter. It so happened that on one occasion, she dropped one of her implements and recited the supplication of *bismillāh* (in the name of Allah) before raising it anew. Because she was a monotheist and refused to accept Fir'awn's claim of divinity, the hairdresser and her children were summarily executed by being thrown into a scorching, fire-filled ditch. However, because she was killed as an oppressed and innocent party, Allah honoured her status and conferred her an elegant fragrance that filled the depths of Paradise. This fragrance was so great that it amazed the leader of the Prophets ﷺ himself. On the other hand, evil oppressors and tyrants like Fir'awn will emit a putrid smell, and as a result of their transgressions, they will be barred from smelling the fragrance of Paradise.

The believers of Paradise will be blessed with the privilege of smelling the fragrance of Paradise throughout their stay in the permanent abode; every step or movement that they make will cause the ground beneath them to emit a new round of the pleasant scent. In fact, the believers themselves will release a pleasant musk-like odour every time they burp. In a transmitted report, the Prophet ﷺ is reported to have said: "The incense burners of the people of Paradise will consist of aloe wood, which will perpetually burn and continually increase the pleasant smell of Paradise."

What will further amplify the experience in Paradise is the pleasant and moderate temperature level that will endure perpetually; the weather will never become too warm or too cold. Any rounds of rainfall will be pleasant and light, which means that the believers will not have any of their travel plans or expeditions outside disrupted by sudden torrential downpours or other forms of inclement weather. Moreover, the Prophet ﷺ is reported to have said: "Whilst we are in Paradise, a cloud possessing that which no eye has ever seen and no ear has ever heard of will come over us. The people will say to the cloud:

أَمْطِرِي عَلَيْنَا

'Pour rain upon us.'"

The Prophet ﷺ mentioned that the cloud will respond to the request of the believers and say:

مَا تُرِيْدُوْنَ أَنْ أُمطِرَكُمْ

"What would you like me to rain upon you?"

The Prophet ﷺ then stated: "It will then rain upon you whatever you wish and however much you desire. Then Allah will send a harmless wind and it will spread heaps of musk on both their right and left sides. It will then come on their faces, hair, and garments. And it will please them in such a way that they will continue to increase in terms of beauty."

There is some discussion amongst scholars and theologians concerning whether or not Paradise will have regular day and night cycles, as experienced in this world. In this regard, the famous exegete al-Qurṭubī ﵀ said: "The scholars have said that there is no night and day in Paradise, and instead they will be in an everlasting and eternal light." The believers will only be aware that a day has come to an end when a special set of curtains and screens are drawn. These covers will then be drawn down during the day, which serves as a signal that the main activity hours are in motion. There are some narrations which suggest that the believers will wear different garments during these different timepoints, with one set reserved for the main hours of the day and another for the later hours as well. In the Qur'an, Allah states the following concerning the nature of Jannah:

لَا يَرَوْنَ فِيهَا شَمْسًا وَلَا زَمْهَرِيرًا

"[In it they will feel] neither [the] heat of the Sun nor intense cold."[22]

[22] *al-Insān*, 13.

In an important narration, Imam Simāk ﵀ reported that he came to the city of Medina and visited the noble Companion ʿAbdullāh ibn ʿAbbās ﵄ after the latter had aged and lost their eyesight. During his visit, Simāk asked Ibn ʿAbbās ﵄ concerning the nature of the ground of Paradise. Ibn ʿAbbās ﵄ replied by stating: "It consists of the white marble of silver, as though it is a mirror." Then Simāk asked: "And what is the light of Paradise?" In response, Ibn ʿAbbās ﵄ said: "Have you ever seen the light right before sunrise? Its light shall be of that nature, except that there will be no Sun nor any cold." This fascinating report begs the question: where does this light come from and how will it endure for eternity? Regarding this fundamental question, Ibn Taymiyyah ﵀ said:

وَالجَنَّةُ لَيْسَ فِيهَا شَمْسٌ وَلَا قَمَرٍ وَلَا لَيْلٌ وَلَا نَهَارٌ، وَلَكِنْ تَعْرِفُ البُكْرَةَ
وَالعَشِيَّةِ بِنُورٍ يَظْهَرُ لَهُمْ مِنْ قِبَلِ العَرْشِ

"In Jannah, there is no night and day, nor any sun or moon. Instead, the morning and evening will be known from a light that appears from the Throne of Allah."

If Ibn Taymiyyah's deduction is correct, then this means that the light of Paradise will come from the Throne of Allah, which is situated in a higher plane. The permanent state of luminescence in Jannah obviously raises some questions, such as whether or not the believers situated within it will ever sleep.

This question was actually raised to the Prophet ﷺ, who in response said:

النَّوْمُ أَخُو الْمَوْتِ وَأَهْلُ الْجَنَّةِ لَا يَنَامُوْن

"Sleep is the brother of death, and the people of Jannah do not die."

In this world, an individual may personally love sleep and use it as a means to relax and dissolve their anxieties and perplexities. Because the Hereafter is free from any such troubles and difficulties, the notion of sleep in and of itself ultimately becomes a meaningless proposition. Within the permanent abode of bliss, the mind, body, and soul will all be in a peaceful and tranquil state. In the temporal world, the believer would resist the desire for sleep during the night and would instead perform the *tahajjud* prayer. In Paradise, Allah will ensure that all those sacrifices and commitments are handsomely recompensed, such that a person will be able to enjoy every single moment in Paradise without the need for any rest.

8

The Gardens of Jannah

Two different gardens of Paradise are found in this world. These two spiritual realms consist of the following: (1) the venues in which Allah's name is remembered and exalted; (2) and the sites where someone else is remembered for the sake of Allah. At first sight, a person may challenge this claim, as it appears extraordinary and devoid of evidence. But it has been established that the Prophet ﷺ said: "The circles of knowledge in this life are gardens of Paradise." This is because the attendee of such blessed gatherings receives the praise of Allah and His Angels, and also raises his spiritual rank with every supplication or litany that he recites. Likewise, in another Hadith, the Prophet ﷺ is reported to have said: "When you go and visit a sick person, 70,000 Angels accompany you and Allah gifts you with a garden consisting of many fruits in Jannah." When we go and visit the sick, we often give them elegant bouquets of flowers in order to cheer their spirits, without realising that Allah will give us a rich and elegant garden that contains a myriad of flowers. As such, the one who praises Allah and becomes cognisant of His presence, as well as the person who remembers their brother for the sake of their Creator, will both be conferred luscious gardens in Paradise.

As noted in the previous chapters, the occupant of Paradise will be granted a myriad of palaces and houses, which they will be able to visit and enter whenever they wish. But will they be allotted other structures of beauty as well? The answer is that they will in fact be provided other elegant residences as well. For instance, outside their palaces, the believers will be provided a myriad of *khiyām*, which in worldly terms can be described as constituting guest houses. Regarding these beautiful structures, Imam Ibn Qayyim al-Jawziyyah ﵀ said: "These *khiyām* are different from the *ghuraf* (special rooms), apartments and palaces found in Paradise. Instead, they constitute pavilions that are situated in the gardens, beach shorelines, and the river fronts of Jannah. The pavilions are designed for guests for the purpose of enjoyment." Ibn Abī al-Dunyā ﵀ has a similar yet different understanding of the nature and purpose of the *khiyām*. In his explanatory note concerning these structures, he states: "All of the heavenly creatures reside in these guest homes, and the palaces are the structures where only the believers live. So, this is what is built for the believers with the permission of Allah."

Ibn Abī al-Dunyā's position is supported by the following Qur'anic verse:

حُورٌ مَقْصُورَاتٌ فِي الْخِيَامِ

"[They will be] maidens with gorgeous eyes, reserved in pavilions." [23]

This verse constitutes a conclusive form of evidence that the special maidens of Paradise—who are known as the *ḥūr al-ʿīn*—will reside within the *khiyām*. Outside these special structures will be a number of servants and housekeepers, who will immediately attend to any of the needs and requests of the believers, regardless of the time of day. At the same time, they will refrain from entering any of the structures to ensure that the privacy needs of the believers are met. With the *khiyām* and the *ghuraf*, the believers will enjoy the privilege of holding special *majālis* with their close fellows and friends. During these sessions, the privacy of the believers will be fully maintained, and no outside actors will be able to witness their exchanges and interactions. In an authentic tradition, the Prophet ﷺ said: "In Paradise, the believer will have a tent made up of a single hollowed-out pearl that spans 60 miles. And as he visits the families and the guests in every one of them, no one will be able to see the other." A number of the early Muslim commentators—such as Ibn ʿAbbās and Ibn Masʿūd ؓ—state that this tent will consist of a hollowed-out pearl of epic proportions, whereby it will approximate the length of one *farsakh* and the width of 50 *farsakhs*. This is undoubtedly an

---

23 *al-Raḥmān*, 72.

The Prophet ﷺ said: "When Jibrīl would strike the ground in Paradise, fragrance would come out." Thus, with every increasing step the believer will actually amplify their experience in Paradise, as more fragrance will be diffused in the air around them.

incredible figure, since a *farsakh* roughly corresponds to five miles. It is also reported that these *khiyām* will possess more than a thousand golden gates, with each and every one of them having an Angel stand before them. These Angels will have special gifts in their possession, which they will give to the believer during specific moments assigned by Allah. These exquisite guest houses will also be furnished with luxurious beds, which the believers can rest on whenever they desire:

مُتَّكِـِٔينَ عَلَىٰ فُرُشٍۭ بَطَآئِنُهَا مِنْ إِسْتَبْرَقٍۚ وَجَنَى ٱلْجَنَّتَيْنِ دَانٍ

"Those [believers] will recline on furnishings lined with rich brocade. And the fruit of both Gardens will hang within reach."[24]

Moreover, later on in the same *sūrah*, Allah states:

مُتَّكِـِٔينَ عَلَىٰ رَفْرَفٍ خُضْرٍ وَعَبْقَرِيٍّ حِسَانٍ

"All [believers] will be reclining on green cushions and splendid carpets."[25]

In another *sūrah* of the Qur'an, the pleasures and bounties of the *khiyām* are outlined in further detail:

فِيهَا سُرُرٌ مَّرْفُوعَةٌ وَأَكْوَابٌ مَّوْضُوعَةٌ وَنَمَارِقُ مَصْفُوفَةٌ وَزَرَابِيُّ مَبْثُوثَةٌ

"...along with thrones raised high, and cups set at hand, and cushions lined up, and carpets spread out."[26]

---

24 *al-Raḥmān*, 54.

25 *al-Raḥmān*, 76.

26 *al-Ghāshiyah*, 13–16.

Taking all these aforementioned verses into account, one can enumerate the following blessings associated with the *khiyām*: (1) golden doors; (2) green drapes; (3) lined-up cushions; and (4) expansive rooms in terms of both height and width.

The religious texts concerning Jannah assign it an exotic character, which ultimately implies that it will be replete with luscious plants and trees, bodies of water, and sandy marshes. Of course, another prevailing theme of Paradise is undoubtedly its myriad of exquisite gardens, whose flora and fauna will please all onlookers. The believer will be able to marvel at the various wonders and beauties of the natural and structural elements before them for as long as they wish, since no temporal restrictions will exist.

At this point, it would be worthwhile to analyse some of the specific elements of Paradise. There are some reports which provide insights concerning the nature of Paradise's soil. In one report, it is related that the Prophet ﷺ said: "The gravel of Jannah consists of pearls and rubies, and the dirt of Jannah is made of saffron." Another Hadith concerning the same topic states: "Its dirt consists of saffron, but its soil is made of musk." Imam Ibn al-Qayyim ﷺ harmonised these two apparently contradictory reports by arguing that whilst the colour of the soil will be that of saffron, its fragrance will be like musk. Such a mode of variation is certainly within the realm of possibility, as Jannah's terrain will not be of a homogenous nature. Ibn al-Qayyim ﷺ justified his stance by stating: "This is the best combination since it constitutes the best form of beauty and radiance."

Interestingly, in some narrations, the Prophet ﷺ states that the ground surface of Paradise will consist of pure white musk. This may be read to imply that Jannah will consist of more than one surface, with each subsequent one being more beautiful than the one that precedes it. One can thus visualise Paradise as comprising of milky-white planes and marshes which will emit the most pleasant fragrance imaginable. This point can be appreciated greater once one considers what the blessed Prophet experienced during the miraculous night journey of al-Isrā' wa al-Mi'rāj. After ascending to Paradise, the Prophet ﷺ said: "When Jibrīl would strike the ground in Paradise, fragrance would come out." Thus, with every increasing step the believer will actually amplify their experience in Paradise, as more fragrance will be diffused in the air around them. But musk and saffron will not be the only substances exuding scents in the permanent abode of bliss. In another Hadith, the Prophet ﷺ confirmed that there will also be hills and dunes made of camphor. In the same report, he ﷺ states: "The people will gather around these hills and dunes. Once they are gathered, Allah will bring upon them breezes of mercy that will continue to diffuse upon them."

The Companions of the Prophet ﷺ were enthralled by these powerful images of Paradise, and they were well aware that the gardens found in it were unlike any plants and vegetation that they witnessed in this world. For this reason, they were eager to perform as many acts of good in order to obtain a spot in Paradise.

In this regard, one may cite a fascinating story concerning the noble Companion Abū Ṭalḥah ﵁. Upon hearing the verse:

لَن تَنَالُوا۟ ٱلْبِرَّ حَتَّىٰ تُنفِقُوا۟ مِمَّا تُحِبُّونَ

"You will never achieve righteousness until you donate some of what you cherish"[27]

He rushed to the Prophet ﷺ and said: "O Messenger of Allah, I have this garden of mine in Medina, and it is the most prized garden in the city." This massive estate—which encompassed several trees and springs—was known as *bi'r ḥā'* and was adjacent to the *masjid* of the Prophet. Abū Ṭalḥah ﵁ provided the rationale for his generous act by stating: "I could not think of anything more beloved to me than this, so I am giving away this garden." He gave up his garden in this *dunyā* (temporal world) so he could possess a permanent garden in Paradise.

A similar event occurred when the noble Companion Abū al-Daḥdāḥ ﵁ heard the following Qur'anic verse:

مَن ذَا ٱلَّذِى يُقْرِضُ ٱللَّهَ قَرْضًا حَسَنًا فَيُضَـٰعِفَهُۥ لَهُۥ

"Who will lend to Allah a good loan which Allah will multiply many times over?"[28]

---

[27] *Āl 'Imrān*, 92.

[28] *al-Baqarah*, 245.

Moved by the message embedded in this verse, Abū al-Daḥdāḥ ﵁ immediately headed to the Prophet ﷺ and said: “This is a garden of 600 palm trees that I am giving for this garden from Allah.”

After returning back to his estate, Abū al-Daḥdāḥ ﵁ noticed that his wife and child were picking dates from the garden he had just given away in charity. He rushed towards his wife and said: “O Umm al-Daḥdāḥ, leave this garden, for I have sold it for a garden in Jannah.” Upon hearing this, Umm al-Daḥdāḥ immediately retrieved all the dates that were in her son’s hand—lest he eat any of them—and said:

رَبِحَ البَيعُ رَبِحَ البَيعُ رَبِحَ البَيعُ

“This is a profitable trade, this is a profitable trade, this is a profitable trade!”

The Prophet ﷺ himself was amazed at this entire episode and said: “How many bundles of date palms in Jannah are for Abū al-Daḥdāḥ!” As Muslims, we can have gardens in Jannah prepared for us by imparting useful and sacred knowledge to others, providing aid to the weak and marginalised folk, and donating a portion of our earnings to the poor and impoverished.

Occupants of Paradise will be granted a myriad of palaces and homes. They will enjoy exquisite guest houses (*khiyām*) with golden doors, green drapes, lined-up cushions and expansive rooms furnished with luxurious beds and angels bearing gifts.

9

How to Plant Trees in Jannah

It is reported that on one occasion, a fascinating incident occurred between the Prophet Sulaymān (عليه السلام) and an old worshipper. Allah had granted Sulaymān (عليه السلام) a mighty army which contained within its ranks a myriad of species, such as birds, insects, jinn, and of course humans. It so happened that on a particular day, Sulaymān (عليه السلام) and his impressive army passed by an ascetic, who was awestruck by the splendour and glory of this Prophet's retinue. The worshipper was so impressed that he actually addressed Sulaymān by saying:

يَا ابْنَ دَاوُدَ لَقَدْ آتَاكَ اللَّهُ مُلْكاً عَظِيماً

"O son of Dāwūd, Allah has given you a magnificent kingdom."

After hearing this worshipper's remark, Sulaymān ﷺ immediately ordered his army to halt and turned towards the man. In his reply, he said:

لَتَسْبِيحَةٌ فِي صَحِيفَةِ مُؤْمِنٍ خَيْرٌ مِمَّا أُعْطِيَ ابْنَ دَاوُدَ، وَ إِنَّ مَا أُعْطِيَ ابْنَ دَاوُدَ يَذْهَبُ وَ التَّسْبِيحَةَ تَبْقَى

"Indeed even a single tasbīḥah (litany of Allah's glorification) from any believer is better than everything that has been given to the son of Dāwūd. And let it be known that everything that has been given to the son of Dāwūd will perish, but this tasbīḥah of yours will remain forever."

The previous chapters of this work established that a believer is able to have trees and gardens planted in their name for performing acts of good in this *dunyā* (temporal world). This section will explore how the believers will harvest their rewards and accrue their corresponding dividends in the Hereafter. During the interdimensional night journey of al-Isrā' wa al-Mi'rāj, the Messenger of Allah ﷺ met the noble Prophet Ibrāhīm ﷺ, who said:

يَا مُحَمَّدُ، أَقْرِئْ أُمَّتَكَ مِنِّي السَّلامَ وَأَخبِرْهُمْ أَنَّ الجَنَّةَ طَيِّبَةُ التُّرْبَةِ عَذْبَةُ المَاءِ، وَأَنَّهَا قِيعَانٌ وَأَنَّ غِرَاسَهَا سُبْحَانَ اللَّهِ وَالحَمْدُ لِلَّهِ وَلَا إِلَهَ إِلَّا اللَّهُ وَاللَّهُ أَكْبَرُ

"O Muhammad, convey to your ummah my salām (greeting of peace), and inform them that Jannah consists of a land whose soil is pure and water is sweet. It consists of a smooth white plain whose trees are planted by saying subḥānallāh (glory be to Allah), alḥamdulillāh (all praise is due to Allah), lā ilāha illā Allāh (there is no God but Allah), and Allāhu akbar (Allah is great)."

Thus, a person can plant a tree in their name in the gardens of Paradise simply for reciting a litany that glorifies Allah and remembers His name. Unfortunately, it is common to find many Muslims squandering much of their spare moments and failing to capitalise on the immense rewards that are found in these simple supplicatory words. But as members of the true faith, it is imperative for us to appreciate the benefits embedded with these words and the various trees and plants that will be allotted to the believers.

The Qur'an and Sunnah provide vivid descriptions of the luscious trees and plants that are found in Paradise. Perhaps the smallest specimen that is mentioned in this regard consists of aromatic herbs, which exude refreshing scents and awaken the senses of the people around them. In one Qur'anic verse discussing the bounties of Paradise given to the believer, Allah states:

فَرَوْحٌ وَرَيْحَانٌ وَجَنَّتُ نَعِيمٍ

"...then [such a person will have] serenity, fragrance, and a Garden of Bliss."[29]

The word that is used to refer to fragrance in this context is *rayḥān*, which is often used to refer to herbal plants that exude sweet smells. Due to the pleasant odours that they exude, these plants are known for their incredible ability to relax the mind and inculcate a state of absolute tranquility.

---

[29] *al-Wāqiʿah*, 89.

As such, the believers will find themselves fully satisfied and free of all the worries and anxieties that are found in this world. Yet, if these benefits are found amongst the plants of Paradise, the trees of the permanent abode of bliss will undoubtedly be superior in terms of the psychological and physical wonders that they will impart to the believers. In fact, in one authentic Hadith, the Prophet ﷺ is reported to have said: "The trees of Paradise are made of gold." Moreover, in one report, it is related that Ibn 'Abbās ‎رضي الله عنه described the aforesaid trees to be emerald green in their structure, whilst also adding that their leaves will be a mixture of red and gold. This latter report is fascinating, since in worldly terms, the trunk is usually the most unattractive component of the tree. But in Paradise, it will possess a glittering emerald green hue that will dazzle all of its onlookers. In a parallel fashion, the other parts of the tree will be equally alluring, such as the branches and the leaves. This point has been succinctly encapsulated in the following Qur'anic verse:

ذَوَاتَآ أَفْنَانٍ

"[Both of the gardens will contain trees] with lush branches."[30]

Thus, in Paradise the believers will not only enjoy the sight of these wonderful trees, they will be able to eat their luscious fruits, which will include pomegranates and dates. In other words, not only will these trees be aesthetically appealing to the eye, they will bear fruits of the best quality. The state of

---

[30] *al-Raḥmān*, 48.

perfection that characterises the trees of Paradise in both these aspects is clearly articulated in the following set of verses:

فِي سِدْرٍ مَّخْضُودٍ وَطَلْحٍ مَّنضُودٍ وَظِلٍّ مَّمْدُودٍ وَمَآءٍ مَّسْكُوبٍ
وَفَٰكِهَةٍ كَثِيرَةٍ لَّا مَقْطُوعَةٍ وَلَا مَمْنُوعَةٍ

"[They will be] amid thornless lote trees, clusters of bananas, extended shade, flowing water, and abundant fruit—never out of season nor forbidden."[31]

Such a description is extraordinary and goes beyond the regular conventions of this world. It is reported that on one occasion, a Bedouin went to the Prophet ﷺ and said: "O Messenger of Allah, Allah has mentioned a tree in Paradise that causes us to become deranged. And I do not think that there is a tree that causes more harm to people than this tree." In response, the Messenger of Allah ﷺ asked: "What type of tree are you referring to?" The Bedouin said: "The *sidr* (lote) tree causes us to lose our minds due to the thorns that it contains." The Prophet ﷺ addressed his concern by stating: "Does Allah not say,

سِدْرٍ مَّخْضُودٍ

'...thornless lote trees...'?"[32]

Such a fact was shocking, since the Arabs had never witnessed a lote tree that was devoid of thorns. In fact, not only did

[31] *al-Wāqiʿah*, 28–33.

[32] *al-Wāqiʿah*, 28.

the Prophet ﷺ state that these trees will be free of any obstructions, he also mentioned that Allah will substitute every single thorn with a fruit instead. Another type of fruit that will be found in Paradise is the banana. Interestingly, it is said that Imam Mālik ﷺ enjoyed regularly consuming bananas, with the noble jurist explaining his affection towards the fruit by noting that it is one of the fruits of Jannah. But even in this world, the banana is a blessed fruit, and it is for this reason that it can be found during every time of the year.

Other tree specimens are particularly described and quantified in the Prophetic Sunnah. For instance, in the Qur'an we are told of a tree that provides *ẓill mamdūd* (extended shade). But the exact dimensions of this tree are not elucidated within the Qur'anic corpus. But the Prophet ﷺ answered this question by noting that there is a tree in Paradise which is so wide that a swift horse rider would require 100 years to traverse it completely. A group of scholars champion the view that this particular tree likely bears the title of Ṭūbā. The word bears similar connotations to the term al-Kawthar, which refers to glad tidings. However, in particular contexts the former can denote a special tree in Paradise, just as the term al-Kawthar can specifically refer to the blessed Ḥawḍ (Pool). The specific denotation of Ṭūbā is arguably intended in the following Hadith:

طُوبَى لِلْغُرَبَاء

"Ṭūbā is promised for the strangers."

According to the specific reading of this Hadith, the believers will be handsomely recompensed with a beautiful and permanent tree known as Ṭūbā in Jannah due to their renunciation of this lowly world. To ensure the attainment of this beautiful tree in the Afterlife, the believer must interact in this world like a stranger: they should view their time here as a mere stay over that culminates with their arrival at the permanent abode. In another Hadith, the Prophet ﷺ repeated the following declaration seven times:

طُوبَى لِمَنْ رَآنِي وَآمَنَ بِي وَطُوبَى لِمَنْ لَمْ يَرَنِي وَآمَنَ بِي

"Ṭūbā is promised for the one who saw me and believed in me, and Ṭūbā is promised for the one who did not see me yet still believed in me."

Ṭūbā bears much significance in Islamic theology, since not only is it a massive tree in Paradise, but it also produces the material that will be used for the clothing of the people of Paradise. In an authentic tradition, the Prophet ﷺ said: "Ṭūbā is a tree in Paradise whose shade encompasses the journey span of a hundred years. And the clothes of the people of Paradise are derived from the outer parts of its flowers." Upon hearing this, a Bedouin addressed the Prophet ﷺ by asking: "Are the clothes woven or are they created?" The attendees and members of the congregation who heard this question began to laugh. The Prophet ﷺ gently rebuked the congregation for ridiculing a perfectly valid question, and explained that the garments will actually grow from the branches of these trees.

Another major tree that will be found in Paradise is known as Shajarah al-Shuhadā', which is designated for the martyrs. This is confirmed in the Sunnah, for there is an authentic Hadith which states that the souls of the believers will metamorphosise into green birds and will be perching on the trees of Paradise. The souls of the martyrs will have their own specific tree, which they will remain upon until the Day of Judgement. On the Day of Judgement, the souls of the martyrs will be further honoured, as they will attain the protection of the shade of Allah's throne.

There is yet another exceptional tree that requires mention in this context, since it is situated in the apex point of the created Universe. This lote tree is known as Sidrah al-Muntahā, which lies at the highest boundary point of Jannah. Other than the site where Sūrah al-Muddaththir was revealed, Sidrah al-Muntahā specifically represents the location where the Prophet ﷺ witnessed the Archangel Jibrīl ؑ in his original form. Once they reached this blessed tree during the interdimensional night journey of al-Isrā' wa al-Miʿrāj, Jibrīl ؑ stared upwards and was in awe at the light and overwhelming force that he sensed from above. He could not ascend any further, as the pressure that was being imposed from above completely barred his mobility. Whilst being at this point of high ascent, the Prophet noted that this special tree's fruits corresponded to the size of the earthenware jars of Hajar, whilst its leaves were like the ears of elephants; every leaf was so large that it could cover the entire population of this ummah. He also noted that the colours and hues found in this plane were unlike the conventional pigments found in this Earth.

After looking at these reports, some scholars have argued that there is an intricate spiritual connection between the lote trees of this world and the Afterlife. For instance, when one of the daughters of the Prophet ﷺ passed away, he ordered the female washers to wash her with water that was mixed with *sidr* (lote tree leaves) and additionally ordered them to add camphor in the last iteration of the cleansing process. The use of lote tree leaves in the washing ritual of the deceased is telling, since it serves as a reminder of how these very plants will be observed in the Afterlife as well. The way that we use this tree in this world will determine whether we will have access to it in the Hereafter.

In a similar regard, we find some religious texts that invoke the palm tree as a simile to describe the believer's faith. In one key Qur'anic verse, Allah states:

أَلَمْ تَرَ كَيْفَ ضَرَبَ اللَّهُ مَثَلًا كَلِمَةً طَيِّبَةً كَشَجَرَةٍ طَيِّبَةٍ أَصْلُهَا ثَابِتٌ
وَفَرْعُهَا فِي السَّمَاءِ تُؤْتِي أُكُلَهَا كُلَّ حِينٍ بِإِذْنِ رَبِّهَا

"Do you not see how Allah compares a good word to a good tree? Its root is firm and its branches reach the sky, yielding its fruit in every season by the Will of its Lord."[33]

33 *Ibrāhīm*, 24-25.

The tree of faith is always healthy and fruitful, as it bears produce at all times of the year. If a believer emulates this standard in this world, then it will be rewarded with such a tree in the Afterlife, whereby they will enjoy its pleasant shade and easily accessible fruit for all of eternity. In other words, the greater the good deeds a person performs in this world, the greater the frequency of luscious fruits they will obtain in Paradise.

Likewise, in an authentic tradition, the Prophet ﷺ stated that whenever a Muslim pays a visit to their sick brethren in faith, the fruits of Paradise will be harvested in Paradise throughout their stay. All it takes for the accruement of this reward is to physically meet their ailing brother and raise their spirits and levels of optimism. In another Hadith, the Prophet ﷺ said: "I saw a man strolling in Paradise in this world because he saw a branch laying on the ground and removed it from the path." This person will be handsomely rewarded with trees and plentiful shade in Paradise simply because he saw an obstruction in a common path and removed it, lest the passersby face harm from it.

10

The Four Rivers of Jannah

The presence of flowing or running water—such as that observed in rivers and other bodies of water—is proven to have positive psychological benefits, a phenomenon which is dubbed as "the blue mind effect". The Qur'an makes effective use of this concept by almost always pairing the gardens of Paradise with rivers that flow beneath them. With regard to the point of origin of these rivers, the Prophet ﷺ said that four rivers flow from the origin point of Sidrah al-Muntahā. He provided further details concerning the nature of these rivers by stating:

نَهْرَانِ بَاطِنَانِ وَنَهْرَانِ ظَاهِرَانِ

"Two rivers [amongst them] are hidden and two are visible."

The Prophet ﷺ himself sought to uncover the names and natures of these bodies of water. Accordingly, he asked Jibrīl n: "What are these rivers?" Jibrīl ﷺ said: "The hidden rivers—namely the ones that are exclusive to Paradise—are Sayḥān and Jayḥān, whilst the visible rivers are the Nile and the Euphrates."

The Prophet ﷺ then continued to trek within the perimeter of Jannah and made the following observation: "I saw another stream whose banks consisted of the domes of hollow pearls. I then placed my hand in the flowing river and noticed that it was pleasant smelling musk. I then asked Jibrīl ﷺ, 'Who is this for?' He then said: 'This is your Kawthar, which has been granted to you by Allah.'"

The members of the Muslim ummah have not enjoyed the privilege to sense or perceive these heavenly rivers. But they remain connected to them, as the origin of humankind can be traced to Paradise. Likewise, the original foundation of the Nile and the Euphrates is Paradise as well, but they are currently represented imperfectly within the confines of this world. Other scholars state that these two rivers are deemed heavenly since they provided ample assistance to the Prophets and their respective followers. For instance, the Prophet Mūsā ﷺ and his followers were nourished with the water of the Nile, whilst the Euphrates—which is situated in Mesopotamia—supported a myriad of Prophets belonging to Banū Isrā'īl (the Children of Israel) during their missions, journeys, and expeditions. Al-Kawthar, on the other hand, is the blessed

The Prophet ﷺ said that al-Kawthar is a stream in Paradise gifted to him by Allah whose banks are made of gold whilst it flows upon pearls and rubies. Its base consists of musk, whilst its water is whiter than snow and sweeter than honey.

fount of our Prophet ﷺ, and it was granted to him as a source of comfort when his enemies had claimed that he was cut off and deprived of all good. After the Prophet's last son passed away, the prominent members of the Quraysh rejoiced at his loss. But Allah then comforted His Prophet ﷺ by promising him a special river in Paradise, and assured him that it was his enemies who were truly cut off. In a parallel fashion, one finds that after reminding them of the hardships and obstacles found in this world, the Qur'an comforts the believers by promising them rivers in Paradise. Before the believers enter Paradise, they will be granted the blessing of drinking from the Ḥawḍ (Pool), whose water originates from the depths of Paradise and is situated in a special basin outside the gates of Jannah. But once the friends of Allah ﷻ are allowed access into Jannah, they will be able to drink from the fount of al-Kawthar, which is the ultimate delight. In an authentic Hadith, the Prophet ﷺ said that al-Kawthar is a stream in Paradise whose banks are made of gold whilst it flows upon pearls and rubies. He also said that its base consists of musk, whilst its water is whiter than snow and sweeter than honey.

Within Paradise, there are long and extensive rivers which increase in their beauty and richness the closer a person gets to their point of origin. This point was accurately captured by Imam Ibn al-Qayyim ﷻ, who said: "All the rivers of Paradise start with a large body of water and then become a waterfall." Moreover, the Prophet ﷺ said in an authentic report: "When you ask Allah, request al-Firdaws from Him, since it is the pinnacle and most superior portion of Paradise."

The rationale for why one should supplicate for al-Firdaws is exemplified in another Prophetic tradition: "Above it is the Throne of the Most-Merciful, and from it all of the rivers of Paradise flow." Thus, just as all light originates from the peak point of Sidrah al-Muntahā, the blessed water of Paradise stems from there as well. In another report, the Prophet ﷺ said: "Within Paradise there is a sea of water, which is followed by a sea of honey. This is then followed by a large body of milk, which is then succeeded by a large body of wine. And from those large bodies the rivers split off and become divided into numerous streams, such that all the inhabitants of Jannah may enjoy their portion." These pleasurable drinks of Paradise are transferred under dunes of musk, which will allow the believers to drink and enjoy them from the comfort of their residences.

If one carefully evaluates the sacred sources of the Shariah, they will find that Allah ﷻ has divided the water channels of Paradise into two distinct categories: (1) the *anhār* (rivers); (2) and the *ʿuyūn* (springs). Regarding the first group, Allah states:

مَّثَلُ ٱلْجَنَّةِ ٱلَّتِي وُعِدَ ٱلْمُتَّقُونَ ۖ فِيهَآ أَنْهَٰرٌ مِّن مَّآءٍ غَيْرِ ءَاسِنٍ وَأَنْهَٰرٌ مِّن لَّبَنٍ لَّمْ يَتَغَيَّرْ طَعْمُهُۥ
وَأَنْهَٰرٌ مِّنْ خَمْرٍ لَّذَّةٍ لِّلشَّٰرِبِينَ وَأَنْهَٰرٌ مِّنْ عَسَلٍ مُّصَفًّى

"The description of the Paradise promised to the righteous is that in it are rivers of fresh water, rivers of milk that never changes in taste, rivers of wine delicious to drink, and rivers of pure honey."[34]

---

[34] *Muhammad*, 15.

From this verse, one deduces that four different rivers will be found in Paradise, with every one of them being made of a distinct substance: water, wine, milk, and honey. But unlike the faulty reality of this world, every one of these rivers will be perfectly distilled and purified, such that they will not be amenable to any distortion or impairment throughout the course of time. In our present world, water develops a bitter taste if it remains stagnant, milk spoils and develops a sour taste, and honey expires. As for wine, in its worldly form it comes with a myriad of problems. This is why the noble Companion Ibn ʿAbbās ﷺ said: "What does wine give you in this world? It only brings forth drunkenness, causes a headache, induces vomiting, and leads to frequent urination. But when Allah mentions the wine of Paradise, He has purified it of all these maladies. Moreover, the corruption of honey is the inescapable level of impurity that is found in this world. But in the plane of Jannah, every single iota in those rivers remains pure." As such, in light of these transmitted reports, one can firmly come to the conclusion that the rivers of Jannah will perpetually remain in a perfect state and will never be subject to any form of distortion.

In other verses of the Qur'an, Allah ﷻ outlines the wonders and comforts found in the *ʿuyūn*:

إِنَّ الْمُتَّقِينَ فِي ظِلَالٍ وَعُيُونٍ

"Indeed, the righteous will be amid shade and springs."[35]

[35] *al-Mursalāt*, 41.

Moreover, we find the name of a spring specifically outlined in another Qur'anic verse:

إِنَّ ٱلأَبْرَارَ يَشْرَبُونَ مِن كَأْسٍ كَانَ مِزَاجُهَا كَافُوراً عَيْناً يَشْرَبُ بِهَا
عِبَادُ ٱللَّهِ يُفَجِّرُونَهَا تَفْجِيراً

"Indeed, the virtuous will have a drink—flavoured with camphor—from a spring where Allah's servants will drink, flowing at their will."[36]

This spring is assigned the name of Kāfūr, which is the Arabic word for camphor. But in the same chapter we find yet another spring mentioned, whose special drink is paired with a blessed spice that will be consumed in Paradise:

وَيُسْقَوْنَ فِيهَا كَأْسًا كَانَ مِزَاجُهَا زَنجَبِيلًا، عَيْنًا فِيهَا تُسَمَّىٰ سَلْسَبِيلًا

"And they will be given a drink flavoured with ginger, from a spring there, called Salsabīl."[37]

36 *al-Insān*, 5–6.

37 *al-Insān*, 17–18.

Just like the previous spring, this special fountain will have wine gushing forth, but it will have its flavour enhanced with ginger. But there is yet another spring—which is known as Tasnīm—that is specifically designated for the *muqarrabūn* (the ones who are close to Allah ﷻ):

وَمِزَاجُهُۥ مِن تَسْنِيمٍ عَيْنًا يَشْرَبُ بِهَا ٱلْمُقَرَّبُونَ

"And this drink's flavour will come from Tasnīm, a spring from which those nearest [to Allah] will drink."[38]

Only the *muqarrabūn* will enjoy the privilege of drinking purely from the Tasnīm. A number of scholars and commentators assert that other elite classes amongst the believers—such as the *abrār* (pious)—will enjoy the opportunity to drink from the spring of Tasnīm, but the amounts they will receive will be limited and mixed with the contents of other springs. But none of the believers will perceive any disadvantage from this exclusion, since they will all have fresh and breathtaking bodies of water flowing within the depths of their homes, whether in the form of springs or rivers. Unlike the current state of water scarcity and inequality that is found in the temporal world, all the inhabitants of Paradise will have permanent and perpetual access to the best rivers and springs conceivable.

38 *al-Muṭaffifīn*, 27–28.

11

Food and Drink in Jannah

When our beloved mother Khadījah رضي الله عنها went to the blessed Prophet ﷺ to present him a tray of food, Jibrīl عليه السلام descended. He conveyed to the Prophet ﷺ the pleasant news that his wife would have a palace built for her in Paradise, whereby she would be served due to her unwavering support of the Prophet. Likewise, the Prophet ﷺ is reported to have issued the following imperative after entering Medina: "Spread the *salām* (greeting of peace) and feed the people." The people who capitalised on this order and provided moral and financial support will receive boundless rewards in Jannah. Since the Prophet ﷺ has departed from the physical world, we cannot replicate this degree of conformity and service, but nevertheless we can provide emotional and monetary support to our communities and attain the everlasting bounties of Paradise.

When a believer enters Paradise, they will be served whatever dish or meal they wish. All that is needed to acquire their dish is a simple order or request, and instantaneously the chefs of Jannah will comply. Unlike in the case of the temporal world, there will be no limits to what can be requested, as all food orders will be honoured. The conventional limits of nature and scarcity that exist in the present Universe will not apply in the Afterlife. But this series of thought-provoking facts leads to a natural question: will the food of Paradise bear any similarity to the produce and dishes that we consume in this world? This question has been adequately addressed in the Qur'an:

كُلَّمَا رُزِقُوا مِنْهَا مِنْ ثَمَرَةٍ رِزْقًا قَالُوا هَٰذَا الَّذِي رُزِقْنَا مِنْ قَبْلُ

"Whenever provided with fruit, they will say, 'This is what we were given before.'"[39]

This means that the edibles presented to the believers will bear an outer resemblance to the items of food found in the Hereafter. However, once they consume the foods of Paradise, it will become evident to them that the food of Paradise can have no equal in terms of quantity and quality. This is why the noble Companion Ibn 'Abbās ﵄ said: "Nothing [in Paradise] will resemble anything of this world except by name

---

[39] *al-Baqarah*, 25.

and title only." A number of scholars and commentators have also noted that the higher one's status is in Paradise, the more luscious and exotic the fruits will be. They deciphered this point by carefully studying the report of the Prophet's famous night journey. In this tradition, the Prophet ﷺ noted that upon reaching the interdimensional apex point known as Sidrah al-Muntahā, he came across trees and grape vines that were completely indistinguishable in terms of colour and size, whereby they superseded the fruits and vegetations of the temporal world. Upon hearing this, a Bedouin exclaimed with much yearning and pleasure, "O Messenger of Allah, will they have grapes in Paradise?" In response, the Prophet ﷺ said: "Yes." The Bedouin then asked: "How large will a bunch of grapes be in Paradise?" The Prophet ﷺ said: "A month-long distance for a flying crow which flies continuously and never becomes tired." Every time the believer plucks a fruit, it will be replenished thereafter automatically. Moreover, the mere desire to consume a particular fruit will cause its tree branches to be lowered, such that a person may pluck it with ease. This will be the handsome recompense for the believers, who sacrificed much of their health and wealth in the temporal world to defend Allah's religion and celebrate His word.

During their eternal stay in Paradise, the believers will be nourished with an endless array of exquisite prepared meals and dishes. In fact, immediately after entering Paradise, the winners of eternal salvation will be provided a delicious appetiser. In one fascinating and thought-provoking Hadith, the Prophet ﷺ said: "Allah will take the entire land of assembly from the

Day of Judgement, transform it into a single loaf of bread, and then have it thrown to them for their consumption." In another report, the Prophet ﷺ was asked: "What will be the welcoming meal in Paradise?" The Prophet ﷺ said: "At this moment there is a bull grazing in Jannah, and it will be sacrificed upon the arrival [of the believers]." In another report, he added that another gourmet dish would be served: "[It will be] a whale whose liver's caudate lobe will be able to feed 70,000 people." Within the communities of Jannah, this special dish will be formally known as *kabid al-ḥūt* (whale liver). Whilst these descriptions may not seem particularly appealing from a worldly viewpoint, it is important to note that the foods of Paradise will be conferred the most delightful of fragrances and flavours, such that they will satisfy all of the believers. In an upper and indiscernible dimension, these delicacies—such as the bull and the whale—are currently being held and cultivated for the people who profess Allah's Oneness.

Another delicacy that will be offered to the believers is the grilled meat of exotic birds. In this regard, Allah states:

وَلَحْمِ طَيْرٍ مِّمَّا يَشْتَهُونَ

"...and [they will be served the] meat from any bird they desire."[40]

In Paradise, the ornamental sky will be glittered with massive and prominent birds that will fly continuously, as they wait to be eaten by the inhabitants of Paradise; whenever a person

---

[40] *al-Wāqiʿah*, 21.

sets their gaze on one of them and wishes to consume them, their meat will be grilled and prepared as they wish, without any effort or time being required in the process. Regarding their size, the Prophet ﷺ said: "Their necks are like the necks of camels." Upon hearing this, the noble Companion 'Umar ibn al-Khaṭṭāb ؓ exclaimed: "What blessed birds!" But in response, the Prophet ﷺ said: "Yet the ones who eat them are even more blessed."

The Jannah experience will be further amplified with a glamorous buffet, which will be garnished with a variety of dishes and meals. Regarding the splendour of this momentous event, Ibn al-Qayyim ؒ states: "70 dishes of gold will be passed around them. Each dish will have a different type of food that is not found in the other." What will even further amplify the experience is that these delicious meals will be presented in golden trays and cups, and a myriad of servants will be dispatched around the believers to provide them with any requested services. For instance, in one key verse, Allah states:

يُطَافُ عَلَيْهِم بِصِحَافٍ مِّن ذَهَبٍ وَأَكْوَابٍ

"Golden trays and cups will be passed around to them."[41]

The servants will carry these ornamented drinks in a special set of vessels known as the *abārīq* (pitchers), which will provide the exact amount desired by every believer. These drinks will be carefully arranged and consist of various combinations

---

41 *al-Zukhruf*, 71.

of the rivers and springs of Jannah. As noted in the previous chapter, some of these drinks will have their flavour enhanced with camphor, whilst others will be supplemented with ginger. In another Qur'anic verse, we learn that another well-matured alcoholic beverage will be fortified with pure musk:

يُسْقَوْنَ مِن رَّحِيقٍ مَّخْتُومٍ خِتَامُهُ مِسْكٌ ۚ وَفِي ذَٰلِكَ فَلْيَتَنَافَسِ الْمُتَنَافِسُونَ

"They will be given a drink of sealed, pure wine, whose last sip will smell like musk. So, let whoever aspires to this strive."[42]

These drinks will be unlike anything that has been observed in this lowly world, for not only will musk be an edible substance, the wine served in the Afterlife will not yield any adverse effects, such as intoxication or clouded judgement. But in order for this optimal state of affairs to be obtained, one must exercise restraint and abide by the divine ordinances. Our beloved Prophet ﷺ underscored this very point when he said: "Do not drink in the vessels of gold and silver and do not eat in their plates. It is for them [i.e., the disbelievers] in this world and for you in the Hereafter." In another Hadith, he said: "Whoever drinks wine in this world will not drink it in the Hereafter." Thus, in light of these reports, we are subject to a number of restrictions and must only consume what has been permitted by our Lord. But by exercising perseverance and making the necessary sacrifices in this world, we will enjoy endless pleasures in the other world.

---

42 *al-Muṭaffifīn*, 25–26.

12

Your Clothing in Jannah

Regardless of its elegance or fabric type, every single article of clothing will eventually wear down with the vicissitudes of time. Interestingly, in a tradition the Prophet ﷺ likened *īmān* (faith) to a garment's long-term condition by stating:

إِنَّ الإِيمَانَ لَيَخْلَقُ فِي جَوْفِ أَحَدِكُمْ كَمَا يَخْلَقُ الثَّوْبُ،
فَاسْأَلُوا اللهَ أَنْ يُجَدِّدَ الإِيمَانَ فِي قُلُوبِكُمْ

"Surely faith wears out in your heart in the same manner that a garment does, so ask Allah to renew the faith in your hearts."

Individuals who have been subscribers to the Muslim faith for extended periods often find their *īmān* lacking its lustre and strength as time progresses—if their faith was represented by a garment, it would likely be torn and ripped. One should thus strive to maintain their faith by re-internalising religious doctrines and developing a strong grasp of Islamic teachings. That way, the garment of faith will remain in an acceptable state and they will be able to attain Paradise in the Hereafter.

When a person enters into Paradise, they will be adorned with the finest and most elegant of garments. This can be inferred from a Hadith where the Prophet ﷺ addressed men by stating: "Whoever wears silk in this world will be barred from it in the Hereafter." In another tradition, it is reported that he ﷺ said: "Whoever wears gold in this world will not wear it in the Hereafter." These narrations share parallels with the Prophetic report that confirms that "whoever drinks wine in this world will not drink it in the Hereafter". The key overarching element found in all of these reports is that a person must abstain from certain sensual pleasures in this world in order to attain them in the Hereafter. The blessed garments of the Afterlife are outlined in a number of verses, such as the following:

وَجَزَاهُم بِمَا صَبَرُوا جَنَّةً وَحَرِيرًا

"...and [He will] reward them for their perseverance with a Garden and [garments of] silk."[43]

[43] *al-Insān*, 12.

The people of Paradise will have bracelets of gold and silver, garlands of pearl and ruby, and the crowns of kings on their heads. Just one pearl from the dress of a woman of Paradise would light up everything between the East and the West.

Just a few verses later in the same chapter, we find Allah state:

عَٰلِيَهُمۡ ثِيَابُ سُندُسٍ خُضۡرٞ وَإِسۡتَبۡرَقٞۖ وَحُلُّوٓاْ أَسَاوِرَ مِن فِضَّةٖ وَسَقَىٰهُمۡ رَبُّهُمۡ شَرَابٗا طَهُورًا

"The virtuous will be in garments of fine green silk and rich brocade, and adorned with bracelets of silver, and their Lord will give them a purifying drink."[44]

In his commentary on this verse, Imam Ibn al-Qayyim ﵀ states that the aforementioned garments are outer layers of clothing that are added to the baseline level of adornment that one is already provided after entering Paradise. In other words, these green garments are not provided for the purpose of concealing the body or one's private parts, but instead they are hallmarks of one's eminent rank and status in Paradise. Ibn al-Qayyim ﵀ also notes that the verse highlights how the beautification of a person's inner and outer states will be achieved through the purifying drink and exquisite garments respectively. The believer who enters Paradise will have all traces of filth and impurity removed by bathing in its blessed rivers, but now they will have their rank further amplified with these special drinks and robes. Both will be provided in perfect proportion without any unnecessary excess or damaging deficiency.

---

[44] *al-Insān*, 21.

As the Qur'an explicitly mentions, the believers will be further decorated with golden bracelets, precious jewels, and stones:

جَنَّاتُ عَدْنٍ يَدْخُلُونَهَا يُحَلَّوْنَ فِيهَا مِنْ أَسَاوِرَ مِن ذَهَبٍ وَلُؤْلُؤًا ۖ وَلِبَاسُهُمْ فِيهَا حَرِيرٌ

"They will enter the Gardens of Eternity, where they will be adorned with bracelets of gold and pearls, and their clothing will be silk."[45]

In fact, just like in the case of their food and palaces, the believers will be continuously served by a jeweller who will ensure that the gems and bracelets of the believers are shaped appropriately and are free of distortions. This perfect process is actually in motion in the present moment. In this regard, Kaʿb al-Aḥbār ﵁ said: "Allah has created an Angel who is assigned the duty of shaping the jewellery of the people of Paradise until the Day of Judgement." In fact, Kaʿb stated that if just a single bangle of the people of Paradise were to appear in this world, it would eclipse the light of the Sun. It is a pity to find that innumerable individuals in this world exercise dubious tactics to hoard the gold of this world, which they will not be able to benefit from in the next world. Such individuals fail to appreciate the fact that a single ounce of gold in the Afterlife supersedes the entire temporal universe and all its riches. The Prophet ﷺ himself confirmed this reality when he said: "If the mere amount of a fingernail of Paradise's extent were to become apparent to the people of this world, it would have beautified the entirety of the

---

45 *Fāṭir*, 33.

heavens and the Earth. And if a man amongst the people of Paradise were to appear and his bracelets were made apparent, it would blot out the light of the Sun." Another report that is related in this regard states: "One pearl from the dress of a woman of Paradise would light up all that is between the East and West." Moreover, another Hadith on the same topic says that the inhabitants of Paradise "will have bracelets of gold and silver, garlands of pearl and ruby, and they will have the crowns of kings on their heads".

In Paradise, the crowns of the believers will vary in size and quality depending on their account of deeds. Undoubtedly, the greatest crown will be the one bestowed upon the *ḥāfiẓ* (memoriser) of the Qur'an and their parents. Regarding this special class of believers, the Prophet ﷺ stated: "The parents of the person who memorised the Qur'an will be dressed in two robes, whose value will exceed everything in this world." Upon being adorned with these exclusive garments, the parents will exclaim: "O our Lord, why are we being given this?" It will then be said to them: "It is due to your child learning the Qur'an." In a similar fashion, the *shahīd* (martyr) will be honoured with a striking and glittering crown. It is related from al-Miqdād ibn 'Amr that a "crown of honour will be placed upon the head of the *shahīd*. One ruby of that crown is better than this world and everything that is within it".

The experience in Jannah will be further amplified with the provision of precious implements and tools. For instance, the believers will be supplied with golden combs for brushing their hair, whereby they will amplify their beauty with every single stroke. Moreover, they will be given exquisite brands of perfume that will render their musk-scented bodies even more fragrant.

But in order for us to be conferred these wonderful garments in the Afterlife, we must ensure that our conduct and morals meet the standards set by our Creator. In a metaphorical sense, we should function as garments who protect our fellow brothers in faith from external harms whilst also concealing their faults. Moreover, we must ensure that we safeguard and comfort our spouses just like how a dress covers a person's body. By leading a life of altruism and benevolence towards one's fellow co-religionists, a person will be rewarded with the priceless dresses of Paradise.

ادْخُلُوهَا بِسَلَامٍ آمِنِينَ

(It will be said to the believers)

"Enter (Jannah) in peace and security."

AL-ḤIJR, 46

The parents of the memoriser of the Qur'an will be dressed in two luxury robes, whose value will exceed everything in this world. The martyr will wear a glittering crown of honour. One ruby of that crown is better than this world and everything that is within it.

13

Making a Wish in Jannah

ʿAbdullāh ibn Masʿūd ؓ related that the Prophet ﷺ said: "I have seen the very last person to exit the Hellfire and enter Paradise." The status and story of this individual—who remains unnamed—is worthy of analysis since they likely committed many misdeeds during their life and only had the baseline level of faith to qualify as a Muslim. After receiving a lengthy amount of punishment in the Hellfire, they will be deemed purified and attain eligibility for Paradise. This person will exit the Hellfire whilst crawling and reduced to a scorched state; they will praise Allah for His deliverance, and then will receive His order to enter the gardens of Paradise. But upon entering Jannah, he will be disappointed to find that all the palaces and residences have already been occupied by the rest of the believers. Thus, he will turn back to Allah ﷻ and state:

يَا رَبِّ قَدْ أَخَذَ النَّاسُ المَنَازِل

"O my Lord, the people have occupied all the residences."

Essentially, this man will be expressing his frustration and bewilderment at his current plight, as he will be without any residence and unaware of what course of action to take. Allah will respond to his complaint by stating: "Do you have any recollection of your past existence and state?" Through this question, Allah will ask the man whether he was aware of the duration of his stay in the Hellfire, and if he could recall his time in the temporal world. The man will reply in the affirmative and remember the bounties and pleasures that he experienced in the *dunyā* (temporal world). Allah will then say to him: "Make a wish." After some reflection, the man will say: "I wish for something, and that is the entire kingdom of the world." In other words, he will wish to possess the accumulated riches of the greatest kingdoms and empires throughout the entirety of human history. From our vantage point, this appears to be an ambitious request, but Allah's generosity has no limits. For this reason, He will say:

لَكَ الَّذِي تَمَنَّيْتَ وَعَشْرَةَ أَضْعَافِ الدُّنْيَا

"You will have that which you wished for,
as well as the entire world ten times over."

This response reflects the benevolence and love of our Creator, since He is decreeing all these bounties for a man who has the lowest level of faith and is the last to enter Paradise. In fact, his entrance will be deferred so much that he will not be able to find any vacant quarters or residences in Jannah. Despite being in such a disadvantaged state, Allah will grant him a wish and honour his request. The man will at first be surprised by this positive response, and even say:

يَا رَبِّ أَتَسْتَهْزِئُ مِنِّي وَأَنْتَ رَبُّ العَالَمِينَ

"O my Lord, are You making fun of me,
when You are the Lord of the worlds?"

At this point, Ibn Masʿūd ﷺ—who was the narrator of the Hadith—began to laugh. Such a sight surprised the listeners, who naturally demanded an explanation. Ibn Masʿūd ﷺ in turn said: "This is because the Prophet ﷺ started to laugh here, and he laughed so much that you could see his back teeth." The Prophet ﷺ explained his laughter by noting that Allah Himself will laugh at hearing the aforementioned response of the servant. Allah will explain that He is not making fun of him:

إِنِّي لَا أَسْتَهْزِئُ مِنْكَ وَلَكِنِّي عَلَى مَا أَشَاءُ قَادِرٌ

"I am not making fun of you, but I am indeed
capable of doing anything I will."

With this beautiful response, Allah will indicate that He is not mocking the man, but instead His conferral of these bounties is a pure manifestation of His divine will. As such, the man will be granted a vast kingdom within the grounds of Paradise, wherein he will dwell forever.

But once all the believers are in Jannah, what activities will they partake in, and how will they spend their time? When addressing this question, the Qur'an provides us a number of general guidelines by indicating that Allah will not disappoint His servants and will provide them with that which pleases them. But it is also important to note that to some extent, the experiences of the inhabitants of Paradise will differ, as every person will have their own wishes and desires. The Qur'an indicates that these responses will be honoured without any restrictions. In one verse Allah states:

وَفِيهَا مَا تَشْتَهِيهِ ٱلْأَنفُسُ وَتَلَذُّ ٱلْأَعْيُنُ ۖ وَأَنتُمْ فِيهَا خَٰلِدُونَ

"There will be whatever the souls desire and the eyes delight in. And you will be there forever."[46]

Moreover, in another verse, Allah says:

وَلَكُمْ فِيهَا مَا تَشْتَهِىٓ أَنفُسُكُمْ وَلَكُمْ فِيهَا مَا تَدَّعُونَ

"There you will have whatever your souls desire, and there you will have whatever you ask for."[47]

46 *al-Zukhruf*, 71.
47 *Fuṣṣilat*, 31.

Regarding the activities of the people of Paradise, there are a myriad of texts which confirm that the people will be granted the opportunity to perform the activities and undertakings that they enjoy. Abū Hurayrah رضي الله عنه related that on one occasion, a Bedouin happened to attend one of the discourses of the Prophet ﷺ. In this session, the Prophet ﷺ related how one of the entrants of Paradise will wish to live the life of a farmer, such that he will cultivate and harvest different crops. Such an experience may appeal to some people and bring them much pleasure. The Prophet ﷺ mentioned that Allah will positively respond to the request of this man and will cause the requested crops to grow in a matter of seconds, with the produce being harvested and reaped before their eyes. Allah will then address the man by saying: "Take whatever you like, O son of Adam, for nothing seems to satisfy you." Upon hearing this magnificent report, the Bedouin exclaimed: "O Messenger of Allah, this person must be from the Quraysh or the Anṣār, since unlike us, they are almost exclusively interested in farming." This rather blunt statement caused the Prophet ﷺ to laugh. In a similar fashion, 'Ikrimah رضي الله عنه narrated that if a person of Paradise merely thinks of cultivating a plot of land in Paradise, the Angels will immediately greet them and say: "Your Lord states that you had a desire in your heart and He knew it, so He sent us with the seeds." The man will then provide instruction on where and how the seeds should be planted.

In Paradise, a person will be able to enjoy certain events and milestones that they were not able to achieve in the temporal world. For instance, a woman who was barren during her worldly life will be able to experience both pregnancy and the birth of her own child, without any complications or discomfort. In a notable Hadith, the Prophet ﷺ confirmed that the process will be painless and efficient, with the exact time period being a matter of their own choice:

الْمُؤْمِنُ إِذَا اشْتَهَى الْوَلَدَ فِي الْجَنَّةِ، كَانَ حَمْلُهُ وَوَضْعُهُ وَسِنُّهُ فِي سَاعَةٍ كَمَا يَشْتَهِي

"If the believers desires to have a child in Paradise, the pregnancy, delivery, and weaning will all occur in the timespan that they desire."

There is a question of whether the inhabitants of Paradise will be able to undertake actions or activities that go against the *fiṭrah* (natural disposition), such as fulfilling unnatural desires. On this question, one cannot find any specific answers. But it is imperative for one to know with full certainty that Allah will ensure all the believers will be pleased and contented. It is possible that these desires may be removed in the Afterlife, whereby a person will no longer have any longing or inclination to perform them. Instead, Allah may instil in the hearts of the believers the desire to perform acts that are even more pleasant and beneficial for them.

14

Your Family in Jannah

A person can never satisfactorily celebrate a major event or achievement without the presence of their family. This ultimately means that being accompanied by one's family in Jannah is imperative. Without having one's family members in near proximity, a person will not be able to feel complete joy. This point is beautifully alluded in the following verse of the Qur'an:

جَنَّٰتُ عَدْنٍ يَدْخُلُونَهَا وَمَن صَلَحَ مِنْ ءَابَآئِهِمْ وَأَزْوَٰجِهِمْ وَذُرِّيَّٰتِهِمْ

"...the Gardens of Eternity, which they will enter along with the righteous amongst their parents, spouses, and descendants."[48]

---

[48] *Ra'd*, 23.

But in order for one to enter Paradise in the first place, it is necessary for them to treat all their family members in a manner that is consistent with Allah's ordinances. The primary example that can be mentioned in this regard is one's parents. On one occasion, a young man approached the Prophet ﷺ and said: "O Messenger of Allah, I wish to go out and fight alongside you." The Prophet asked him: "Do you have a mother?" The man said: "Yes." The Prophet ﷺ then said:

فَالْزِمْهَا فَإِنَّ الجَنَّةَ تَحْتَ رِجْلَيْهَا

"Then go and stay with her, for Paradise lies beneath her feet."

Similarly, in another incident, a man came to the Prophet ﷺ and sought to fight as a warrior in the Muslim army but said, "O Messenger of Allah, I left my parents crying." The Prophet ﷺ addressed this man by stating: "Then go back to them and make them laugh the same way that you made them cry." In addition, in another notable Hadith, the Prophet ﷺ said that the father is the middle gate of Jannah. As such, a person must consistently exert their best efforts to please their parents, since they represent the main path to Paradise.

Spouses that had turbulent relationships in this worldly life will have all their hurtful memories erased from their recollection, and will instead lead tranquil and loving lives within the confines of Paradise.

If this sincere endeavour is made, they will reunite in the most blessed of planes: Paradise. In this regard, Allah says:

وَالَّذِينَ آمَنُوا وَاتَّبَعَتْهُمْ ذُرِّيَّتُهُم بِإِيمَانٍ أَلْحَقْنَا بِهِمْ ذُرِّيَّتَهُمْ وَمَا أَلَتْنَاهُم مِّنْ عَمَلِهِم مِّن شَيْءٍ ۚ كُلُّ امْرِئٍ بِمَا كَسَبَ رَهِينٌ

"As for those who believe and whose descendants follow them in faith, We will elevate their descendants to their rank, never discounting anything of the reward of their deeds. Every person will reap only what they sowed."[49]

This beautiful verse reflects the mercy of Allah. Generally speaking, different accounts of deeds lead to the conferral of different stations and ranks in Paradise; this *prima facie* should lead to the separation of parents and children. But despite the differences in deeds and levels of righteousness between the different members of a family line, Allah will still ensure that they are united in the same plane of Paradise. Regarding this fascinating phenomenon, the noble Companion Ibn ʿAbbās ﵄ said: "Allah will raise the offspring of the believer to the same degree as them, even if they are lower than them in terms of good deeds; this is because such a result brings joy to the heart of Allah's servant." To illustrate this point, Ibn ʿAbbās ﵄ recited the aforementioned verse. He then continued, saying: "So, if the parents are higher, Allah will put them at ease by bringing the children higher. And if the children are higher, then Allah will join them at the higher level. But Allah will never decrease the rank of anyone out of His mercy and generosity." Interestingly,

[49] *al-Ṭūr*, 21.

some scholars have said that this intergenerational parity extends to one's grandparents, great-grandparents, and other believing ancestors as well. To make things even better, all of one's believing descendants will be present as well in the same spatial sphere, even if they happened to be born hundreds of years after one's death. But what further amplifies the experience is that the believer will be gifted with the opportunity to intercede on behalf of family members who lack the sufficient quantity of deeds to enter Paradise. As for relatives who passed away in a state of disbelief, intercession will not be possible. But the believer will not feel any distress due to their absence, since Allah will eliminate all sadness from the hearts of the inhabitants of Paradise.

In Jannah, every single person will have a spouse, even if they happened to be single during their time on this Earth. The Prophet ﷺ is confirmed to have said: "No individual will be single in Jannah." Moreover, in the Qur'an Allah states:

ادْخُلُوا الْجَنَّةَ أَنتُمْ وَأَزْوَاجُكُمْ تُحْبَرُونَ

"Enter Paradise, you and your spouses, rejoicing."[50]

The spouses will be beautified beyond measure and given perfect forms:

إِنَّا أَنشَأْنَاهُنَّ إِنشَاءً فَجَعَلْنَاهُنَّ أَبْكَارًا عُرُبًا أَتْرَابًا

"Indeed, We will have perfectly created their mates, making them virgins, loving and of equal age."[51]

---

50 *al-Zukhruf*, 70.

51 *al-Wāqiʿah*, 35–37.

Spouses that had turbulent relationships in this worldly life will have all their hurtful memories erased from their recollection, and will instead lead tranquil and loving lives within the confines of Paradise. As the Prophet ﷺ confirmed in a beautiful Hadith, the moment a person enters Jannah, all their anxieties and points of apprehension will dissolve instantaneously. In a similar fashion, all the imperfections and misgivings that existed between spouses in this world will subside in the eternal abode of bliss. In fact, the loving bonds between a husband and wife will increase exponentially, such that their longing for one another will be intense during any brief point of separation. In this regard, Ibn Abī Lubābah ﷺ relates the following report: "You will miss your spouse 70 times more every time you part from one another, and you will experience that much more joy every time you return to one another."

There are still some outstanding questions which require further analysis. For instance, if a woman had married more than once during her lifetime, which husband will she be paired with in Paradise? On this matter, there are a myriad of opinions. According to one view—which is supported by the majority of scholars—she will be united with her last husband. This position is supported by the fact that the wives of the Prophet ﷺ were prohibited from marrying again after his death. According to a second position held by some theologians and jurists, she will enjoy the opportunity to choose which husband she is accompanied with in the Hereafter. There is also a third view which states that she will be paired with her best husband. Regardless of which opinion turns out to be accurate, there can be no doubt that the quality of companionship and marital bliss in Jannah will be at an unparalleled level.

A believer will also be reunited with their children who passed away at a premature age. In a beautiful Hadith, the Prophet ﷺ said: "The children of the believers will be in Paradise, being cared for by Ibrāhīm and Sārah until they give them back to their parents on the Day of Judgement." In fact, the Prophet ﷺ said the following about his own son Ibrāhīm, who died as an infant: "There is a wet nurse for him in Jannah." These deceased children will thus be kept in a special centre in Paradise, where they will eagerly await the arrival of their parents. The famous ascetic Mālik ibn Dīnār ﵀ is said to have seen his deceased infant daughter in a dream, with the latter waiting for him under a special dune of musk. Our blessed Prophet ﷺ said that the deceased children of the believers will wait for their parents at the gate of Paradise, and once they see them, they will firmly grab them by the hand. They will refuse to let go of them until Allah allows their parents to enter Paradise with them. Once they are reunited in Paradise, the parents will enjoy the opportunity to see their child grow into an adult, a spectacle they could not observe in the temporal world. Just like their parents, they will be at the prime age of 33, dwell happily with their parents for all of eternity, and praise Allah for facilitating their re-unification once more.

The deceased children of the believers will wait for their parents at the gate of Paradise. When they see them, they will firmly grab their hand and refuse to let go until Allah allows their parents to enter Paradise with them.

15

Your Friends in Jannah

A popular aphorism in the Arab world states:

الصَّاحِبُ سَاحِبٌ إِمَّا إِلَى الْجَنَّةِ وَإِمَّا إِلَى النَّارِ

"A friend will either drag you to Paradise or the Hellfire."

This saying serves as a strong reminder that the individuals we befriend in this world will affect our standing in the Hereafter, as they shape and determine our moral conduct and religious standing. One must choose their friends carefully, or otherwise they may be resurrected with people of iniquity and will be forced to remain in the Hellfire with them forever. Conversely, pious and religiously conscious friends are a blessing, since they inspire one to pray, fast, recite litanies, and perform other acts of worship for the sake of Allah. These types of interactions create powerful spiritual bonds, whereby one loves their fellow brother in Islam for the sake of Allah, which is one of the greatest deeds possible.

The noble Successor ʿUrwah ibn al-Zubayr ﵀ once had an emotional and spiritual experience with the Mother of the Believers, ʿĀ'ishah ﵂. He provided the details of this incident by stating: "One day, I went to ʿĀ'ishah—who was my aunt—in order to ask her some questions. I found her standing up, praying, and reading the Qur'an. She was constantly reading a series of verses, crying profusely, and making *duʿā'* (supplication). She was taking so long that I said to myself, 'Let me go shop and do my required errands, and I will return back later when she is finished.'"

After making his necessary purchases in the marketplace, ʿUrwah ﵀ returned to ʿĀ'ishah's home many hours later. Yet, not only did he find her to be still in prayer, he noticed that she was reciting a particular sequence of verses continuously:

وَأَقْبَلَ بَعْضُهُمْ عَلَىٰ بَعْضٍ يَتَسَآءَلُونَ قَالُوٓاْ إِنَّا كُنَّا قَبْلُ فِىٓ أَهْلِنَا مُشْفِقِينَ
فَمَنَّ ٱللَّهُ عَلَيْنَا وَوَقَىٰنَا عَذَابَ ٱلسَّمُومِ

"They will turn to one another inquisitively. They will say, 'Before we used to be in awe in the midst of our people. So, Allah has graced us and protected us from the torment of scorching heat.'" [52]

---

[52] *al-Ṭūr*, 25–27.

This sequence vividly describes how the believers will meet one another in Paradise and recall their time in the world. They will remember how they gathered together to worship Allah, remember Him, and ensure that they were all on the straight path. They will also praise Allah for His generosity and His deliverance, for it was only through His grace that they were rescued from the people of wickedness, and by logical extension, the Hellfire. After holding this intimate conversation, these believers will celebrate their salvation.

The bonds of friendship that existed between the believers in this world will further intensify in Paradise. The Prophet ﷺ said: "Once the people of Paradise enter their abode, the friends that used to worship Allah together will begin to long for one another." To ensure their hearts are even further bonded, Allah will cause their couches—that they are reclining on—to come closer. During their discussions, they will identify the exact point in this worldly life where Allah showered them with His mercy and forgave their sins. For some believers, that pivotal moment will be the Hajj ceremony, whilst for others it will be their prayers and invocations during the 27th night of Ramadan. Such a shared memory between them will be priceless. In another pivotal narration, the Prophet ﷺ said: "Amongst the delights of the people of Paradise will be that they will visit one another on mounts and camels. And they will be supplied with saddled horses that will neither defecate nor urinate. They will be able to ride them wherever they wish by the mercy of Allah." These discussions will not simply include individuals belonging to a given generation, as on many occasions people removed by several centuries will be present as well. In fact, the later Muslims will sometimes be honoured with the opportunity to spend time with the Companions ﵃ that they loved and longed to see.

In many of these circles, the believers will discuss relatively mundane topics, such as reflecting on amusing moments, journeys, and other milestones in their lifetimes. But the people of knowledge and sacred learning will wish to discuss intricate matters pertaining to the religious sciences, such as *tafsīr* (Qur'anic exegesis), *fiqh* (Islamic jursprudence), and the *sīrah* (Prophetic accounts). In this regard, Imam Ibn al-Qayyim ﵀ said: "Imagine the students and seekers of sacred knowledge and how they will continue their discussions in Jannah." But the beauty of these other-worldly discussions is that all mysteries and ambiguities will be resolved. If a person wishes to know the authenticity of a given Hadith or verify a point of the *sīrah*, they will have the opportunity to seek clarification from the Prophet ﷺ directly without any intermediaries coming between them. These individuals will thus have the opportunity to enhance their knowledge and grounding in the Shariah in an unprecedented manner. In the temporal world, they were already reflecting one dimension of Paradise, since the Prophet ﷺ said: "The circles of knowledge are gardens of Paradise in this Earth." But in the Afterlife, this experience will be fully actualised, since their religious circles will actually occur within the gardens of Paradise.

Unfortunately, some friends and loved ones will fail to enter Jannah, and they will be placed in the Hellfire. But thankfully, it is possible to secure their salvation through the mechanism of *shafāʿah* (intercession). Regarding this momentous affair, the Prophet ﷺ said: "There will be people who will enter into Hellfire and remain there perpetually, without dying or living. But there will be others who will enter Hellfire due to their sins and will be burnt until they turn into coals. But then permission will be granted for *shafāʿah*: they will be brought out of it in groups and will then be spread over the side of the rivers of Paradise. It will then be said:

يَا أَهْلَ الجَنَّةِ أَفِيضُوا عَلَيْهِم

'O people of Paradise, pour water over them.'"

After being washed with this blessed water, the charred remains of the people rescued from Hell will grow just like how seeds grow in a valley after a flood. The Messenger of Allah ﷺ said that this washing will cause all the fire burns and marks on their bodies to be removed. After entering Paradise, these newcomers will be labelled with the playful term of Jahannamiyūn (the former inhabitants of the Hellfire) by the forerunners of Paradise.

From this beautiful Prophetic report one can derive a number of benefits. Perhaps the most important point is that every Muslim should strive to be a source of goodness and a wellspring of guidance for the general believing population.

That way, they may intercede on behalf of any friends or associates who enter the Hellfire. Moreover, a person should strive to always be surrounded by good companions who will be able to instil moral growth and protect them from the evil temptations of this world. This explains why the Prophet ﷺ said: "Adhere to the collective group and beware of separation." And if someone wishes to be part of the best group in Paradise, they should love and emulate the path of the Prophet ﷺ and his Companions رضي الله عنهم.

ادْخُلُوهَا بِسَلَامٍ آمِنِينَ

(It will be said to the believers)

"Enter (Jannah) in peace and security."

AL-ḤIJR, 46

16

Seeing Your Enemies in Jannah

The righteous Companion and Caliph ʿUmar ibn al-Khaṭṭāb ﷺ is reported to have said:

لَا يَكُنْ حُبُّكَ كَلَفًا، وَلَا بُغْضُكَ تَلَفًا

"Let not your love for someone be so excessive that you become attached to them, and let not your hate for someone be so excessive that it ends up becoming destructive."

In a similar manner, ʿAlī ibn Abī Ṭālib ﷺ said: "It may be that the person you love most becomes your enemy one day. And it may be that your enemy one day becomes a beloved friend." Taking these statements into consideration, one should not attach their religious faith to a particular personality, lest this figure one day err tremendously and cause their followers to face a moral crisis. Likewise, too much hate towards a particular personality can be toxic and cause one to overlook any good contributions made by the latter. To maintain balance in the matter, one must always attach their love and hate towards personalities purely for Allah's sake, that is, without taking into account any worldly considerations. It is imperative to note that an evil friend may call you to the Hellfire, whilst a wise enemy may propel you towards good and inadvertently cause you to attain Paradise. This latter point has been powerfully captured in the Qur'an. For instance, one may consider the following conversation from Sūrah al-Ṣāffāt, where the dangers of an evil friend are illustrated in elaborate detail:

فَأَقْبَلَ بَعْضُهُمْ عَلَىٰ بَعْضٍ يَتَسَاءَلُونَ

"Then they will turn to one another inquisitively."[53]

This conversation will occur between a group of the inhabitants of Paradise, who will wonder what the fate of a mutual friend was.

[53] *al-Ṣāffāt*, 50.

Allah has promised His aid and assistance for individuals who face persecution and oppression at the hands of tyrants in this world. Islam is thus a religion of justice and ensures that the rights of the oppressed are restored in the Afterlife.

A member of the group will express this point with the others:

قَالَ قَائِلٌ مِّنْهُمْ إِنِّي كَانَ لِي قَرِينٌ يَقُوْلُ اَئِنَّكَ لَمِنَ الْمُصَدِّقِيْنَ ءَاِذَا مِتْنَا وَكُنَّا تُرَابًا وَّ عِظَامًا ءَاِنَّا لَمَدِيْنُوْنَ

"One of them will say, 'I once had a companion [in the world], who used to ask, 'Do you actually believe [in resurrection]? When we are dead and reduced to dust and bones, will we really be brought to judgment?'''"[54]

This friend of his was a rejector of the truth and tried to instil doubts in the hearts of the believers. This concerned Muslim—who is recalling his friend's disbelief—will then say to his peers:

قَالَ هَلْ اَنْتُمْ مُّطَّلِعُوْنَ فَاطَّلَعَ فَرَاٰهُ فِيْ سَوَآءِ الْجَحِيْمِ

"He will ask, 'Would you care to see [his fate]?' Then he will look and spot him in the midst of the Hellfire."[55]

After making inquiries concerning the state of his friend, he ultimately discovers that they have been destined to the lowest depths of the Hellfire. After seeing his friend in this miserable state, he will address them and say:

قَالَ تَاللّٰهِ اِنْ كِدْتَّ لَتُرْدِيْنِ ۙ وَلَوْ لَا نِعْمَةُ رَبِّيْ لَكُنْتُ مِنَ الْمُحْضَرِيْنَ

"He will say, 'By Allah! You nearly ruined me. Had it not been for the grace of my Lord, I would have certainly been amongst those brought [to Hell].'"[56]

---

54 *al-Ṣāffāt*, 51–53.

55 *al-Ṣāffāt*, 54–55.

56 *al-Ṣāffāt*, 56–57.

This believer will thank Allah for His deliverance and the salvation provided to him in Paradise. In fact, he will be so overjoyed with his state of affairs that he will actually ask his fellow peers whether or not Jannah will be a permanent abode, since such a proposition would mean that he would be surrounded by pleasures for all of eternity:

اَفَمَا نَحْنُ بِمَيِّتِيْنَۙ اِلَّا مَوْتَتَنَا الْاُوْلٰى وَمَا نَحْنُ بِمُعَذَّبِيْنَ

"[Then he will ask his fellow believers] 'Can you imagine that we will never die, except our first death, nor be punished?'"[57]

It will soon dawn upon this believer that the gardens of Parade will be a permanent abode that will never be dissolved. As such, he will exclaim:

اِنَّ هٰذَا لَهُوَ الْفَوْزُ الْعَظِيْمُ لِمِثْلِ هٰذَا فَلْيَعْمَلِ الْعٰمِلُوْنَ

"This is truly the ultimate triumph.
For such [honour] all should strive."[58]

A number of exegetes and commentators argue that the two friends mentioned in this sequence are none other than the two companions that are cited in Sūrah al-Kahf. One of these companions was so wealthy and well-to-do that they owned two luscious gardens. However, in light of this immense wealth, this person developed an arrogant disposition; not only did they believe that they were better

---

[57] *al-Ṣāffāt*, 58–59.
[58] *al-Ṣāffāt*, 60–61.

than their companion, they also assumed that they did not need to obey Allah's commandments and prepare for the Hereafter. Because of their abject arrogance, the disbelieving companion was thrown into the Hellfire, whilst their humble friend entered Paradise. There is an alternative opinion—which is supported by a transmitted report—that the two individuals mentioned in Sūrah al-Ṣāffāt were actually business partners, with each of them having their own unique orientation and outlook on life. Whilst one of them was righteous and conscious of the divine, the other was hedonistic and materialistic. According to the narration supporting this view, the two men successfully executed a transaction that yielded 8000 dinars of profit, with the accrued amount being equally split between them. The gluttonous partner began to use the wealth to invest in lucrative enterprises; for instance, he purchased a major plot of land for investment purposes. The religiously-conscious friend, on the other hand, gave a thousand dinars away in charity and invoked: "O Allah! I seek to purchase the land of Jannah." The materialistic partner then proceeded to mock his companion for this course of action, even going as far as dismissing the possibility of there being any riches in Paradise.

Thereafter, the hedonistic man proceeded to spend a thousand dinars from his earnings to purchase a home. His religious friend, on the other hand, gave an additional thousand dinars in charity and said: "O Allah! I am giving away a thousand dinars and I am seeking a home in Paradise."

The materialist party once again chastised his counterpart, this time stating that there are no homes in Paradise. Thereafter, the self-indulgent businessman proceeded to spend a thousand dinars in order to secure a sensual relationship. The God-conscious partner, on the other hand, gave away another fourth of his earnings for the sake of Allah, asking his Creator to bestow him a spouse in Jannah. Once again, the former rebuked the latter and asserted that no such provisions exist in an otherworldly plane. Then the opulent businessman spent his last thousand dinars to purchase slaves and other status-enhancing products.

Conversely, the religious party gave away the final quarter of his profit in charity and said: "O Allah, I am seeking the servants, material provisions, and adornment of Paradise." Despite being mocked on every single occasion, the righteous man did not hesitate to spend in the path of his Lord, and refused to succumb to the evil suggestions and temptations of his business partner. This story serves as a vivid reminder that people of religion will always be mocked and ridiculed; they will be dismissed as naive individuals who forego the pleasures and gains of this world for the sake of an unobservable Hereafter. But because the believers exercise unwavering faith in Allah and make the sacrifices necessary for attaining salvation, they will be handsomely rewarded in the other world.

Another category of individuals who will be seen suffering in Hellfire are the tyrants and oppressors of this world. Allah has promised His aid and assistance for individuals who face persecution and oppression at the hands of tyrants in this world, saying: "I swear by My might, I will come to your aid, even if it is after some time." Islam is thus a religion of justice and ensures that the rights of the oppressed are restored in the Afterlife. In fact, whilst in Paradise, the believers will be able to witness the suffering of the oppressors in Hell through special outlets and see-through panels. Regarding this fascinating spectacle, Kaʿb ﷺ stated: "Between Paradise and the Hellfire there are peepholes. When a believer wishes to look at his oppressor from this world, he may do so through one of those peepholes." Such a sight will please the believer, as it will be a confirmation that all their prayers and supplications for Allah were heard and positively answered.

One of the rather strange spectacles in Paradise will be the meeting of former foes and belligerents, with each of the two sides being surprised to see the other in the abode of bliss. Concerning this fascinating occurrence, the Prophet ﷺ said: "When the murderer and the murdered meet in Paradise, Allah laughs at them." For instance, one may consider the epic scene of Ḥamzah ibn ʿAbd al-Muṭṭalib ﷺ—the uncle of the Prophet—meeting his killer Waḥshī ﷺ, who accepted Islam later in his life. Or alternatively, one may imagine the martyrs of the Battle of Uḥud meeting Khālid ibn al-Walīd and ʿIkrimah ibn Abī Jahl ﷺ, who were still non-Muslims during the time and played a decisive role in routing the Muslim army during the later stages of the contest. However, later on in their lives they accepted Islam and led the Rāshidūn army to a number of victories against the Roman and Persian empires.

The two sides will meet one another in a cordial and gracious manner, with no hostility and indignation existing in their hearts. This is because they will all be united with the cord of faith, as demonstrated in their collective salvation.

Even individuals who engaged in disputes and quarrels will reconcile after being reunited in Paradise. In this matter, one may mention the tragic dispute that occurred between the forces of ʿAlī ibn Abī Ṭālib and ʿĀ'ishah ﷺ in the Battle of the Camel, which culminated with the deaths of Ṭalḥah ibn ʿUbayd Allāh and Zubayr ibn al-ʿAwwām ﷺ. Neither of the two sides wanted such bloodshed to occur, but a group of troublemakers and dissidents from the two sides stirred a conflict between the two camps. The death of these beloved Companions immensely disturbed ʿAlī ﷺ, who washed Ṭalḥah ﷺ and prayed over him. After the funeral prayer had concluded, ʿAlī ﷺ rose and addressed the people by saying: "Some of the people claim that only the fools came out to fight, but in actual fact the most honoured faces on Earth came out." After honouring Ṭalḥah's name with this moving speech, ʿAlī ﷺ narrated that he heard the Prophet ﷺ say:

طَلْحَةُ وَالزُّبَيْرُ جَارَايَ فِي الجَنَّةِ

"Ṭalḥah and Zubayr are my neighbours in Paradise."

Then 'Alī ﷺ said, "I ask Allah to make you and me amongst those who are mentioned in the verse:

وَنَزَعْنَا مَا فِي صُدُورِهِم مِّنْ غِلٍّ إِخْوَانًا عَلَىٰ سُرُرٍ مُّتَقَابِلِينَ

'We will remove whatever bitterness they had in their hearts. In a friendly manner, they will be on thrones, facing one another.'"[59]

As such, they will all enter Paradise in a cheerful and tranquil state, without there being any resentment in their hearts.

(It will be said to the believers)

"Enter (Jannah) in peace and security."

AL-ḤIJR, 46

---

[59] *al-Ḥijr*, 47.

17

Thrones and Couches in Jannah

In this world, the believers exercise a life of humility and *taqwā* (God-consciousness). This means that they avoid the trappings of wealth and power as much as possible. The thrones of this world are almost always reserved for the tyrants and oppressors. Obviously, the believers detest those figures, and as such will prefer a life of debasement in order to attain prestige in the sight of their Lord ﷻ. Their main objective is to maintain a humble lifestyle that does not interfere with their ultimate goal of attaining salvation in the Hereafter. They are well aware of the fact that true wealth and honour is found in Paradise, since the delights in that domain will be everlasting.

In Paradise, the believers will be honoured with decorated and bejewelled chairs and thrones. The provision of such chairs will provide them the opportunity to finally rest after toiling in the temporal world for many years. The majestic thrones indicate the bestowal of perpetual honour, a status which none of the monarchs and leaders of the world could possess. In addition, the houses of the believers will be further beautified with prominent beds, elegant and colourful drapes made of silk, and exquisite carpets. Many of these divine allotments are explicitly mentioned in the Qur'an:

فِيهَا سُرُرٌ مَرْفُوعَةٌ وَأَكْوَابٌ مَوْضُوعَةٌ وَنَمَارِقُ مَصْفُوفَةٌ وَزَرَابِيُّ مَبْثُوثَةٌ

"...along with thrones raised high, and cups set at hand, and cushions lined up, and carpets spread out."[60]

In a similar fashion, another verse of the Qur'an states:

مُتَّكِـِٔينَ عَلَىٰ رَفْرَفٍ خُضْرٍ وَعَبْقَرِيٍّ حِسَانٍ

"Those believers will recline on furnishings lined with rich brocade."[61]

A common theme that is found in these verses is the elimination of *hamm* (anxiety), which explains why the believers will be able to comfortably recline and be at ease. In the temporal world, the souls of the Muslims were not able to rest, since they were fearful of their fate in the Afterlife.

60 *al-Ghāshiyah*, 13–16.

61 *al-Raḥmān*, 54.

People who love one another for the sake of Allah will be positioned in prominent rooms and platforms in Paradise. They will appear to be shining stars to the lower-ranking members of Paradise.

Besides being able to rest on elaborate cushions and couches, the believers will also enjoy the opportunity to attend special gatherings before their Creator ﷻ. The elite camp of the believers will be erected on platforms of light. They will be followed by believers who will be resting on platforms of gold and silver. The lowest camp will be sitting on a sheet that is made of pearls. Despite these disparities, the Prophet ﷺ said: "No one will assume that their counterpart is higher than them." From their respective gathering points, the believers will be able to clearly observe their Lord, just as an onlooker in this world can perceive the full Moon in the clear sky. Nothing will match such a blessing, for one will be addressed directly by Allah without any intermediary, whilst they remain comfortably seated on a platform that represents their rank. These special cushions will remain forever in their respective positions, thereby providing the believers the opportunity to enjoy the optimal point of Jannah whenever they wish. Regarding this special privilege, Imam Ibn al-Qayyim رحمه الله states: "The description of the cushions and carpets being lined up and spread demonstrates that they will be always available for you to recline and sit upon. And they will be never hidden nor taken away from you." This everlasting state of bliss is unlike the resorts and hotels of the temporal world, in which the special chairs and cushions are removed after some point of time.

Another factor which will further amplify the Jannah experience is the intimate intergenerational discourses between the believers. This source of enjoyment has been elaborately described in the Qur'an:

ثُلَّةٌ مِّنَ الْأَوَّلِينَ وَ قَلِيلٌ مِّنَ الْآخِرِينَ عَلَىٰ سُرُرٍ مَّوْضُونَةٍ مُّتَّكِئِينَ عَلَيْهَا مُتَقَابِلِينَ

"They will be a multitude from earlier generations, and a few from later generations. All will be on jewelled thrones, reclining face to face."[62]

This will be a pleasant and awesome setting, since the later generations of the Muslims will be able to have close and intimate conversations with the best of people, such as the Companions رضي الله عنهم and the Successors رحمهم الله. Their thrones will be close to one another, with each person directly facing their counterpart. Every side will be able to relate specific events and occurrences in their own generation, with precious moments of history being shared in this blessed setting.

There will be other prominent gatherings attended by individuals who forgave each other for the sake of Allah. As confirmed in the Qur'an, such individuals enjoy an eminent rank and standing:

وَنَزَعْنَا مَا فِي صُدُورِهِم مِّنْ غِلٍّ إِخْوَانًا عَلَىٰ سُرُرٍ مُّتَقَابِلِينَ

"We will remove whatever bitterness they had in their hearts. In a friendly manner, they will be on thrones, facing one another."[63]

62 *al-Wāqi'ah*, 13–16.

63 al-Ḥijr, 47.

Because these individuals possess pure hearts and untroubled souls, they will enjoy an elevated rank in Paradise. But according to a sound Hadith, there will be another group of believers who will enjoy a higher position than them: the believers who love one another for the sake of Allah. Regarding this latter group, Ka'b ﷺ said: "The people who love one another for the sake of Allah will be positioned in prominent rooms and platforms in Paradise. This will be to the extent that will appear to be shining stars to the lower-ranking members of Paradise, who will say:

هَٰذَا رَجُل مِّنَ الْمُتَحَابِّيْنَ فِي اللهِ

'This must be one of the people who loved their contemporary for the sake of Allah.'"

This report should inspire us all to attain this high rank, since by doing so we will be sources of light and will be admired by others.

18

Raising Your Rank in Jannah

The Prophet ﷺ is the best of examples, and his actions and statements in all facets of life constitute standards of goodness that we should aim to emulate. Likewise, the Companions of the Prophet ﷺ were all champions and paragons of true faith, and as such they are models that we should aspire to follow. Islam is not a religion that promotes mediocrity, but instead it inspires us to follow the path set by the Prophet ﷺ and Islam's early forerunners.

That way, one will be rewarded with a higher rank in Jannah. In this regard, Allah says:

وَلِكُلٍّ دَرَجَاتٌ مِّمَّا عَمِلُوا

"They will each be assigned ranks according to their deeds."[64]

Thus, a person's deeds will determine their *manāzil* (stations) in the Afterlife; the various levels in Paradise and Hell are known as *darajāt* (degrees of goodness) and *darakāt* (degrees of evil) respectively. Deeds will also play an instrumental role in entering the abode of bliss, for some scholars state that the invocation that will have to be recited in order to enter Jannah is *lā ilāha illā Allāh* (there is no God but Allah). Every single level of Paradise is vast in its breadth, with its dimensions being so large that it can incorporate the entirety of humankind. But as champions of the truth, we must always aim to attain the highest level.

This naturally leads to the following question: how does a person ensure that they possess an elevated rank in Paradise? This query is addressed in the following verse of the Qur'an:

وَلِمَنْ خَافَ مَقَامَ رَبِّهِ جَنَّتَانِ

"And whoever is in awe of standing before their Lord will have two Gardens."[65]

---

64 *al-An'ām*, 132.

65 *al-Raḥmān*, 46.

Later on in the same chapter, it is interesting to find that another set of gardens are mentioned:

وَمِن دُونِهِمَا جَنَّتَانِ

"And below these two Gardens will be two others."[66]

When looking at these verses holistically, some of the scholars concluded that the first set of gardens will be superior to the second in terms of their station and beauty. This stance can be appreciated if one carefully considers the distinguishing characteristics found in the first set, which include the following:

فِيهِمَا عَيْنَانِ تَجْرِيَانِ

"In each Garden will be two flowing springs."[67]

This will be superior to the second set of gardens, which will only have gushing—and not flowing—springs. Another group of exegetes and interpreters rejected this interpretation. They assert that in actual fact every believer will have two sets of gardens in Paradise: one is allotted for the good deeds they performed in this life, whilst the other is provided for the sins from which they abstained. Whilst all the believers will be bestowed eminent ranks, some will be more elevated than others in light of their virtues and deeds. For this reason, Imam al-Ḍaḥḥāk ﷺ mentioned that the believers who are placed in a higher position will be able to sense and recognise their superior rank. In a Hadith, the Prophet ﷺ

66 *al-Raḥmān*, 62.

67 *al-Raḥmān*, 50.

The sponsorship of orphans and effective parenting are both means of attaining the highest rank in Paradise. Raising a pious and God-fearing child is also undoubtedly one of the best means to obtain salvation in the Hereafter.

stated that this elite class of the believers will be privileged insofar as they will be stationed in *ghuraf* (special rooms) and will appear like stars in the sky. In addition, the Messenger of Allah ﷺ shared a number of guidelines whose adoption will allow one to attain this eminent rank. The Companion Muʿādh ibn Jabal ﷺ narrated that he heard the Prophet ﷺ say: "Whoever performs the five daily prayers, fasts the month of Ramadan, performs the Hajj, Allah will forgive him regardless of whether he partook in the *hijrah* (Islamic migration) or remained in the place that he was born." Upon hearing this, Muʿādh ﷺ said: "O Messenger of Allah, shall I go and tell the people about this?" Muʿādh ﷺ wished to relate this report to his fellow peers so that they may know that performing the minimum baseline of good deeds will suffice for their salvation. But the Prophet ﷺ said: "No Muʿādh, let them strive and toil. For Jannah has 100 degrees, and the distance between every two degrees is like the distance between the heavens and the Earth, with the highest one amongst them being al-Firdaws. And above it is the Throne, and it is the uppermost level of Paradise. The rivers of Jannah flow from that apex point. So, when you invoke Allah, ask Him for al-Firdaws." Thus, a person must never suffice themselves with performing the bare minimum of virtuous deeds, but instead should exert their uppermost efforts towards attaining al-Firdaws. This is because the person who merely undertakes the lowest level of good is bereft of any buffer that may protect them from straying away from the path of goodness.

In the aforementioned Hadith, the Prophet ﷺ mentioned that Jannah consists of 100 degrees. Some scholars—such as Imam Ibn Taymiyyah —opine that this number should not be read literally, since it is used as a literary figure to demonstrate the myriad levels and stations found in Paradise. This is similar to the Hadith which states that Allah has 99 names; this figure was used in a non-literal sense by our beloved Prophet ﷺ, namely to indicate the numerous names and titles of the Creator. Similarly, Ibn Taymiyyah argues that in the former narration the Prophet ﷺ was indicating the numerous levels of Paradise, such that the listeners would be animated and driven to perform good deeds on a continual basis.

In order to obtain the highest level of Paradise, a Muslim must embody and personify the quality of *taqwā* (God-consciousness) in their day-to-day interactions. In this regard, Imam al-Dhahabī said that the people of al-Firdaws are the ones who "cried at night with Allah and smiled at the people during the day". Moreover, this seeker must be a person of action and productivity in terms of supporting the religion of Allah.

The distinguishing characteristics and hallmarks of the people of action are vividly described in the following Qur'anic passage:

لَا يَسْتَوِى الْقٰعِدُوْنَ مِنَ الْمُؤْمِنِيْنَ غَيْرُ اُولِى الضَّرَرِ وَالْمُجٰهِدُوْنَ فِيْ سَبِيْلِ اللّٰهِ بِأَمْوَالِهِمْ وَأَنْفُسِهِمْۗ فَضَّلَ اللّٰهُ الْمُجٰهِدِيْنَ بِأَمْوَالِهِمْ وَأَنْفُسِهِمْ عَلَى الْقٰعِدِيْنَ دَرَجَةًۗ وَكُلًّا وَّعَدَ اللّٰهُ الْحُسْنٰى وَفَضَّلَ اللّٰهُ الْمُجٰهِدِيْنَ عَلَى الْقٰعِدِيْنَ اَجْرًا عَظِيْمًا

"Those who stay at home—except those with valid excuses—are not equal to those who strive in the cause of Allah with their wealth and their lives. Allah has elevated in rank those who strive with their wealth and their lives above those who stay behind. Allah has promised each a fine reward, but those who strive will receive a far better reward than others."[68]

Moreover, there are a number of highly virtuous actions which will allow one to be from amongst the entrants of al-Firdaws. For instance, the Prophet ﷺ said:

أَنَا وَكَافِلُ اليَتِيمِ فِي الجَنَّةِ كَهَاتَيْنِ

"I and the one who takes care of an orphan will be [close to one another] like these two fingers."

He then joined his two fingers. This reward obviously indicates the attainment of al-Firdaws, since the Prophet ﷺ will be granted the highest station in Paradise. In another report, the Messenger of Allah ﷺ said: "Whoever strives to raise two daughters well will be in Jannah like these two fingers."

68 *al-Nisā'*, 95.

As such, the sponsorship of orphans and effective parenting are both effective means of attaining the highest rank in Paradise. Raising a pious and God-fearing child is without doubt one of the best means to obtain salvation in the Hereafter. In an authentic Hadith, the Prophet ﷺ said: "Allah will be raising a person in Paradise, and during their state of elevation the individual will ask, 'O Lord! How am I obtaining all of this?' Allah will say: 'This is because your child sought forgiveness for you.'" Logically, this child only became acquainted with the process of *istighfār* (seeking the forgiveness of Allah) thanks to the religious instruction they received from their parents. Unbeknownst to the parents, the sincere efforts that they exerted towards instilling religious conviction and sincerity in the hearts of their children raised their ranks in the Hereafter.

Likewise, the memoriser of the Qur'an will be honoured with an elevated rank in Paradise, with their exact station and degree being commensurate with the amount they know by heart. This virtue is confirmed in the following Hadith of the Prophet ﷺ: "The reciter of the Qur'an will be told to recite until the very last *āyah* (verse) that they know." The status of the reciter will be further amplified if they recite the divine word of Allah consistently and act upon its teachings. The Messenger of Allah ﷺ said that 10 rewards will be allotted for every single *ḥarf* (letter) of the Qur'an that is read. One can then only imagine how many rewards will be accrued for every verse or passage that is actively implemented.

Another group of believers who will attain the highest level of Paradise are the champions of truth, namely the ones who bore the trials of this world with perseverance and unwavering trust in Allah. The greatest individuals who belong to this category are none other than the *shuhadā'* (martyrs), who fought to defend the faith of Allah on the battlefield; Allah will smile towards them on the Day of Judgement, and will allow them to enter Paradise without any trial or account. Alongside the martyrs will be the individuals who withstood the general trials of this world with perseverance and the firm acceptance of the divine decree. The virtues of this sub-category are elaborately outlined in a Hadith recorded in *Ṣaḥīḥ Ibn Ḥibbān*: "Indeed a man may have a rank in the sight of Allah that he is unable to achieve by virtue of his good deeds. So, Allah will continue to put that person to trial until he reaches the rank that has been designated for him." In other words, in order for a person to be rewarded for exercising unwavering patience, they must be subjected to trials. This conclusion can be inferred from the following Qur'anic verse:

أُولَٰئِكَ يُجْزَوْنَ الْغُرْفَةَ بِمَا صَبَرُوا

"It is they who will be rewarded with mansions for their perseverance."[69]

---

[69] *al-Furqān*, 75.

The last category that can be mentioned amongst the elite believers are the individuals who sincerely and wholeheartedly love Allah and His Messenger ﷺ. ʿĀ'ishah ﵂ narrated that on one occasion a man came to the Prophet ﷺ and said: "O Messenger of Allah, you are more beloved to me than myself and my own family. You are more beloved to me than my children. Sometimes when I am at home and I remember you, I cannot help myself and come towards you and find you. And if I want to see you, I come to the mosque. But, O Messenger of Allah, I remember that there will come a time that I will die; both my death and your death will come. I realise that even if we enter Jannah, you will be in a special plane with the Prophets. I thus fear that even if I enter Jannah, I will not be able to see you anymore." This Companion loved the presence of the Prophet ﷺ more than all the riches and pleasures in this world, but they feared that this priceless source of comfort would be unavailable in the Afterlife. The Prophet ﷺ did not immediately respond to the man's query, and instead sought elaboration from Allah. The following verse was then revealed:

وَمَن يُطِعِ اللَّهَ وَالرَّسُولَ فَأُولَٰئِكَ مَعَ الَّذِينَ أَنْعَمَ اللَّهُ عَلَيْهِم مِّنَ النَّبِيِّينَ
وَالصِّدِّيقِينَ وَالشُّهَدَاءِ وَالصَّالِحِينَ وَحَسُنَ أُولَٰئِكَ رَفِيقًا

"And whoever obeys Allah and the Messenger will be in the company of those blessed by Allah: the prophets, the people of truth, the martyrs, and the righteous—what honourable company!"[70]

70 *al-Nisā'*, 69.

This verse gave the man—who was from amongst the righteous folk and sincerely loved the Prophet ﷺ—glad tidings that he would be reunited with the Prophet ﷺ in the Afterlife. The same conclusion can be inferred from another Hadith, where a man came to the Prophet ﷺ and said: "O Messenger of Allah, the only thing that I have prepared for the Day of Judgement is that I love you." The Prophet gave this man glad tidings by stating:

أَنْتَ مَعَ مَنْ أَحْبَبْتَ

"You will be with the ones whom you love."

Upon hearing this Hadith, Anas ibn Mālik ؓ rejoiced and said: "That is the best thing that I have heard, for I thought to myself, 'I love the Messenger of Allah, I love Abū Bakr, and I love 'Umar.'"

From this report, one key and fundamental benefit may be derived: the best way to obtain the high stations of Paradise is to love the individuals most beloved to Allah, not people of a mediocre or suboptimal rank. As thus, a person will attain the highest rank if they love the Messenger of Allah ﷺ, since he was the best member of all creation. Consequently, in this world, one should love the Prophet ﷺ, emulate his teachings and commandments, and with the permission of Allah, they will be united with him in Paradise.

A person must never suffice themselves with performing the bare minimum of virtuous deeds, but instead they should exert their uppermost efforts towards attaining the highest level of Paradise called al-Firdaws and ask Allah to reach there.

19

The Marketplace in Jannah

In many respects, the current temporary world comprises of a massive and competitive market, in which entrepreneurs aim to promote goods, ideas, and hedonistic notions to the masses. But against this backdrop of materialistic impulses, there is a special group of believers who aim to secure the goods and merchandise that Allah has promised in the Hereafter. This very point was underscored by the Prophet ﷺ, who assured the Anṣār (Helpers) that they would be recompensed in the Hereafter for all the sacrifices they made for the sake of Islam: "The merchandise of Allah is precious, and verily the merchandise of Allah is Jannah."

In Chapter 6, the famous *duʿā’* (supplication) of entering the marketplace was cited, which provides one million rewards, erases one million misdeeds, and raises one's rank by a million degrees. One of the key sections of this virtuous formula states:

يُحْيِي وَيُمِيتُ وَهُوَ حَيٌّ لَا يَمُوتُ

"He gives life and causes death, He is Ever-Living and does not die."

This portion of the supplication is very powerful and serves as a reminder that whilst we may assume that the marketplace is the centre of enrichment and human flourishing, in actual fact it is Allah alone Who provides all animation and happiness in this world. For this reason, a person remembers Allah and glorifies His name so that he may be enriched both spiritually and materially. Moreover, through this supplication we remind ourselves that the Afterlife is exponentially more valuable than anything that is found in this world. Thirdly, this Hadith illustrates to us that Jannah possesses an infinite number of stations and levels, since the Prophet ﷺ said that every time the supplication is made, their status in Paradise will be raised by a million ranks. For this reason, to maximise the number of accrued rewards one should ensure that they recite this supplication every time they enter a marketplace or shopping centre.

If one assesses the Prophetic Sunnah, they will find that there is an interesting juxtaposition drawn between the marketplace and areas of virtue. For instance, in one Hadith, the Prophet ﷺ said: "The most beloved of places to Allah are the mosques, and the most hated of places are the marketplaces." The stark contrast between these two sites lies in the fact that the former are sites of divine remembrance, whilst the latter are areas of heedlessness. Whilst the marketplaces are sites of transient profit, the mosques provide their visitors permanent dividends that will be accrued in the Hereafter. This is why the Prophet ﷺ said: "Every single step that you take to the masjid encompasses the wiping away of sins, the recording of good deeds, and the elevation of your rank in Jannah." Moreover, in an important verse Allah indicates that the observance of prayer in the mosque is a far more profitable undertaking than any financial transaction:

يَٰٓأَيُّهَا ٱلَّذِينَ ءَامَنُوٓا۟ إِذَا نُودِىَ لِلصَّلَوٰةِ مِن يَوْمِ ٱلْجُمُعَةِ فَٱسْعَوْا۟ إِلَىٰ ذِكْرِ ٱللَّهِ
وَذَرُوا۟ ٱلْبَيْعَ ذَٰلِكُمْ خَيْرٌ لَّكُمْ إِن كُنتُمْ تَعْلَمُونَ

"O believers! When the call to prayer is made on Friday, then proceed to the remembrance of Allah and leave off business. That is best for you, if only you knew."[71]

[71] *al-Jumu'ah*, 9.

Thus, one should enter the *masjid* in a state of God-consciousness, tranquility, and full reverence; any time that they spend there and every step they take to reach there will improve their relationship with their Creator and increase their prospects in the Hereafter. Thus, if any conflicts arise between religious and worldly interests, the former should be assigned precedence. This explains why Allah says the following in Sūrah al-Jumuʿah:

وَإِذَا رَأَوْا تِجَارَةً أَوْ لَهْوًا انفَضُّوا إِلَيْهَا وَتَرَكُوكَ قَائِمًا ۚ قُلْ مَا عِندَ اللَّهِ خَيْرٌ مِّنَ اللَّهْوِ وَمِنَ التِّجَارَةِ ۚ وَاللَّهُ خَيْرُ الرَّازِقِينَ

"When they saw the fanfare along with the caravan, they flocked to it, leaving you standing. Say, 'What is with Allah is far better than amusement and merchandise. And Allah is the Best Provider.'"[72]

To illustrate the trappings of wealth and worldly desires, the great Companion Abū Hurayrah ﵁ said: "If meat or money was being distributed in the *masjid*, people would rush to it." Moreover, in a dramatic bid to call the people to the mosque, Abū Hurayrah ﵁ once entered the marketplace and made the following declaration: "The inheritance of the Prophet ﷺ is being distributed in the masjid." Upon hearing this statement, the merchants and customers in the market rushed to the mosque in an attempt to obtain some wealth or merchandise. But the moment they entered the mosque, they were surprised to find that there were no provisions being distributed.

---

72 *al-Jumuʿah*, 11.

Instead, the place of worship was filled with circles of knowledge, where a variety of religious sciences were being taught. They were taken aback by this sight, and sought elaboration from Abū Hurayrah ﵁ as they could not find anything of tangible monetary value being distributed. Abū Hurayrah ﵁ asked them bluntly: "What did you happen to find?" They said: "We found all of these gatherings of knowledge." Abū Hurayrah ﵁ then said: "That is the inheritance of the Prophet ﷺ." In light of this report, one infers that sound sacred knowledge is the inheritance of the Prophet ﷺ; it is more valuable than all the wealth and riches found in this world, since it benefits one both in this world and the Hereafter.

Paradise will possess a special marketplace that is free of all the distractions and materialist impulses of this world. Saʿīd ibn al-Musayyib ﵀ reported that he once happened to cross paths with Abū Hurayrah ﵁, who said to him: "Make *duʿāʾ* that Allah unites us together in the marketplace of Jannah." Ibn al-Musayyib ﵀ was startled by this request, and said: "Is there a marketplace in Jannah?" Abū Hurayrah ﵁ replied by saying: "Yes, indeed. The Messenger of Allah ﷺ informed me that when the people of Jannah enter the abode, they will be placed there in accordance with their deeds. And they will be granted permission to meet Allah on a time period that corresponds to Friday..." Thus, just like in the case of this temporal world, Friday will be the greatest day in Paradise as well, as it will be the day when the believers will gather together in the blessed marketplace and will be blessed with the Beatific Vision. But unlike the case of this world, where one is required to abandon all trade at midday and head to the mosque to perform the Friday prayer, in Paradise the believers will meet one another within the comforts of a great market. Abū Hurayrah ﵁ continued his narration by noting that the Prophet ﷺ said the following concerning this boundless market: "There is this marketplace in Jannah that the people will visit every Friday, and Allah will send a wind that will blow musk on their faces and garments, whereby their beauty and goodness will be amplified. And when they go back home to meet their families, their household members will say to them, 'By Allah, you have increased in beauty and goodness.' And you will then say back to your family, 'By Allah, you too have increased in beauty and in goodness.'" This marketplace will have an unlimited inventory, whereby it will possess every imaginable product or type of produce. Likewise, no person will have a limited budget, as they will be permitted to pick as many products and goods as they wish. Thus, in the perpetual abode of bliss, none of the believers will be subjected to the constraints that conventionally exist in the finite world.

20

Seeing the Companions in Jannah

The most beautiful quarter of Paradise will be the neighbourhood of the Prophet ﷺ, which will include all the honourable members of his pure household, as well as the family lines of other Prophets, such as the household of ʿImrān. The grandsons of the Prophet ﷺ will preside as the leaders of the youth of Paradise, with other Prophets and luminary figures assuming ancillary roles.

In an authentic Hadith, the Prophet ﷺ said:

الحَسَنُ وَالحُسَيْنُ سَيِّدَا شَبَابِ أَهْلِ الجَنَّةِ، إِلَّا ابْنَي الخَالَةِ عِيسَى ابْنِ مَرْيَمَ وَيَحْيَى بْنِ زَكَرِيَّا، وَفَاطِمَةُ سَيِّدَةُ نِسَاءِ أَهْلِ الجَنَّةِ، إِلَّا مَا كَانَ مِنْ مَرْيَمَ بِنْتِ عِمْرَانَ

"Al-Ḥasan and al-Ḥusayn are the two masters of the youth in Jannah, except for the two cousins ʿĪsā ibn Maryam and Yaḥyā ibn Zakariyā. And Fāṭimah is the master of all women in Paradise, except for the case of Maryam, the daughter of ʿImrān."

Maryam عليها السلام is considered an exception due to the high status conferred to her through the following divine address:

إِنَّ اللّٰهَ اصْطَفٰكِ وَ طَهَّرَكِ وَ اصْطَفٰكِ عَلٰى نِسَآءِ الْعٰلَمِيْنَ

"Surely Allah has selected you, purified you, and chosen you over all women of the world."[73]

Thus, the highest station of Paradise will be conferred to the household of the Messenger of Allah ﷺ and the household of ʿImrān. In another important Hadith, the Prophet ﷺ enumerated the identities of the female leaders of Paradise by stating: "The leaders of the women in Jannah are four: Maryam, Fāṭimah, Āsiyah, and Khadījah." Every one of these God-conscious women had their own distinct set of virtues. Maryam عليها السلام was a pure and chaste woman who led a life of worship and countered the false slanders levelled against her through the divine intervention of Allah. Fāṭimah رضي الله عنها

---

[73] *Āl ʿImrān*, 42.

In light of her numerous sacrifices and efforts towards serving Islam, Khadījah رضي الله عنها will be rewarded with an exquisite pearl house in Jannah, in which she will reside with the Messenger of Allah ﷺ.

resembled the Messenger of Allah ﷺ the most in terms of character and physical attributes. Āsiyah ؓ sacrificed all the material comforts found in the palace of Fir'awn in order to maintain her faith in Allah, whilst asking her Creator to build her a superior house in Paradise. Khadījah ؓ was the first female who accepted Islam, and she was the strongest supporter of the Prophet ﷺ during the advent of the mission of the Prophet ﷺ. During the dark pre-Islamic era known as *jāhiliyyah* (lit. the period of ignorance), Khadījah ؓ owned a marvellous mansion which had a breathtaking silk pavilion built right in front of it. She was thus extremely wealthy and played an active role in a number of commercial enterprises. However, even in the days of *jāhiliyyah* she was known for her generosity: not only did she actively support the impoverished people that lived in her vicinity, she also allocated wealth for bachelors so they may marry. In light of her numerous sacrifices and efforts towards serving the faith of Islam, Khadījah ؓ will be rewarded with an exquisite pearl house, in which she will reside with the Messenger of Allah. Āsiyah ؓ and the household of 'Imrān will also be present in this neighbourhood, with every one of them having their own respective mansions. In the same area one will find the residences of the other wives of the Prophet ﷺ, who will be handsomely rewarded with their own specific units (*ḥujurāt*).

Allah has promised the wives of the Prophet ﷺ the best of rewards by addressing them as follows:

وَمَن يَقْنُتْ مِنكُنَّ لِلَّهِ وَرَسُولِهِ وَتَعْمَلْ صَالِحًا نُّؤْتِهَا أَجْرَهَا مَرَّتَيْنِ وَأَعْتَدْنَا لَهَا رِزْقًا كَرِيمًا

"And whoever of you devoutly obeys Allah and His Messenger and does good, We will grant her double the reward, and We have prepared for her an honourable provision."[74]

The great exegete Ibn Kathīr commented on this verse by stating that the promised reward is an allusion to the highest point in Jannah, which is known as *al-'illiyyīn*. The units of the Prophet's wives will be stationed in this special plane, a spectacle which will dazzle all onlookers. In this same area, one will also find the residences of *al-'asharah al-mubashsharūn*—the ten elite Companions who were promised Paradise. This illustrious list consists of the following noble figures: Abū Bakr, 'Umar, 'Uthmān, 'Alī, Ṭalḥah, Zubayr, 'Abd al-Raḥmān ibn 'Awf, Sa'd ibn Abī Waqqāṣ, Sa'īd ibn Zayd, and Abū 'Ubaydah ibn al-Jarrāḥ ﷺ. The leaders of this group will be Abū Bakr and 'Umar ﷺ, and as a result they will be provided superior palaces. During the miraculous night journey of al-Isrā' wa al-Mi'rāj, the Prophet ﷺ traversed the plains of Jannah and came across a prominent golden palace. The Prophet ﷺ assumed that it was built for him, so he asked Jibrīl ﷺ whether he could enter the premises. However, Jibrīl replied by stating: "This is actually the residence of 'Umar ibn al-Khaṭṭāb." When recounting this story, the Prophet ﷺ said: "I then remembered how jealous of a man

74 *al-Aḥzāb*, 31.

'Umar 🙵 was, so I immediately moved away from the residence."
This declaration caused 'Umar 🙵 to weep profusely and say:

أَعَلَيْكَ أَغَارُ يَا رَسُولَ اللهِ

"Can anyone be jealous of you, O Messenger of Allah?"

As for Ṭalḥah and Zubayr 🙵, they will be provided
wonderful palaces in close proximity to the Prophet 🕊. In an
authentic Hadith, the Prophet 🕊 said:

طَلْحَةُ وَالزُّبَيْرُ جَارَايَ فِي الْجَنَّةِ

"Ṭalḥah and Zubayr are my neighbours in Paradise."

These two Companions played a dynamic role in defending the
Prophet 🕊 during the later stages of the Battle of Uḥud. When
the Muslim line broke and the polytheists sought to attack the
Prophet 🕊, al-Zubayr 🙵 advanced forward—sword in hand—
and repulsed their advance. During the same epic battle, Ṭalḥah
stood prominently like a human shield and ensured that all
arrows aimed at the Prophet 🕊 hit him instead. As a result, he
was known as "the walking *shahīd* (martyr)". In the same plane,
one will also find the best members of the *shuhadā'* (martyrs)
from the first generation of Islam, an illustrious list that includes
Ḥamzah ibn 'Abd al-Muṭṭalib and Ja'far ibn Abī Ṭālib 🙵,
who were killed in the battles of Uḥud and Mu'tah respectively.
During the miraculous night journey, the Prophet 🕊 traversed
Jannah and witnessed Ja'far 🙵 flying elegantly in the sky; two
wings assumed the place of his hands, both of which he had
lost during the Battle of Mu'tah. As for Ḥamzah 🙵, he was

seen reclining on an extravagant couch in a blissful state. The Prophet ﷺ observed the residences and servants of other martyrs as well. For instance, during his tour of Jannah, he was welcomed by a young female servant. He asked her: "To whom do you belong?" She said: "I belong to Zayd ibn Ḥārithah." Just like Jaʿfar ibn Abī Ṭālib ﷺ, Zayd ibn Ḥārithah ﷺ was tragically killed in the Battle of Mu'tah whilst leading the Muslim army against the Romans. Another prominent Companion who will also be designated a palace in the apex point of Paradise is none other than Saʿd ibn Muʿādh ﷺ, who was a chieftain of the Anṣār and one of the strongest supporters of the Prophet ﷺ in the battlefield and diplomatic affairs. When Saʿd ﷺ passed away, the Prophet ﷺ said: "The Throne of Allah shook out of joy when the soul of Saʿd returned to it." On a special occasion, the Prophet ﷺ was wearing a beautiful garment that was gifted to him by a foreign monarch. The Companions were taken aback by its elaborate design and elegance. After observing their reactions, the Prophet ﷺ said: "You think that this is beautiful? By Allah, the handkerchief prepared for Saʿd ibn Muʿādh ﷺ in Jannah is better than this garment."

During the Battle of Badr, a young Companion by the name of Ḥārithah ibn Surāqah ﷺ was tragically killed by a fatal arrow strike. His mother was concerned with his fate in the Afterlife, and as such she once approached the Prophet ﷺ and said: "O Messenger of Allah! Inform me of what happened to my son. If he is in Jannah, then I will be patient. But if he is not in Jannah, then I will just continue to mourn." In response, the Prophet ﷺ said: "O Umm Ḥārithah! Jannah does not simply consist of a single level. It is not simply the case that your son has entered Jannah, but he has also ascended to the highest plane known as al-Firdaws al-Aʿlā."

Another category of righteous believers who will be granted access to the highest level of Paradise are the sincere seekers of the truth. A key example of this elite class is the noble Companion ʿAbdullāh ibn Salām ﷺ. Initially presiding as a leading rabbi for the Jewish community in Medina, ʿAbdullāh ibn Salām immediately accepted Islam after the Prophet ﷺ migrated to the city and spread the message of Islam to its inhabitants. In light of his sincere adoption of the faith, the Prophet ﷺ said: "ʿAbdullāh ibn Salām is the tenth of the first ten to enter Jannah." Moreover, in a number of other reports, the Prophet ﷺ gave this Companion the glad tidings of Paradise. Alongside this group, there will be the individuals who championed monotheism as their religious faith but died before the inception of Islam and the Prophetic mission. The main figure that can be mentioned in this category is the monotheist Zayd ibn ʿAmr ibn Nufayl. This man rejected the polytheistic model which dominated the Arabian Peninsula and instead preached the pure unitarian call of Ibrāhīm ﷺ; this was during a time when no one spoke of the oneness of Allah and His sole right to be worshipped. Because of Zayd's firm and unwavering adoption of the true faith of monotheism, the Prophet ﷺ said: "When the various nations are lined up behind their Prophets, Zayd ibn ʿAmr will be a nation by himself." In another narration, the Messenger of Allah ﷺ said: "I entered into Jannah and I found that Zayd ibn ʿAmr ibn Nufayl had two levels of Paradise all to himself."

Another prominent Meccan figure who shunned polytheism and affirmed the oneness of Allah was Waraqah ibn Nawfal. Waraqah was an extremely frail man when the first episode of revelation descended, and he did not have the strength to provide physical support to the call of the Prophet ﷺ. However, he affirmed the Messenger-hood of the Prophet ﷺ and provided him some words of support before his demise. Because of his firm declaration of Allah's oneness, Waraqah will be conferred one of the best stations in Paradise. In a tradition, the Prophet ﷺ said: "Do not speak ill of Waraqah, for I have seen that he has one or two gardens in Jannah all to himself."

Al-Firdaws will also incorporate the believers who diligently served the Prophet ﷺ and glorified Allah's name throughout their lives. The best example of such a figure is none other than Bilāl ibn Rabāḥ ؓ, who will be assigned the title of *sayyid al-mu'adhdhinīn* (the master of the callers) on the Day of Judgement. Regarding Bilāl's status in the Afterlife, the Prophet ﷺ said: "I entered into Jannah and I heard footsteps ahead of me. And I said, 'O Jibrīl, what is that sound?' He said: 'Those are the footsteps of Bilāl.' The scholars explained the astonishing import of this report by stating that in Medina, Bilāl ؓ would precede the Prophet ﷺ by entering the mosque and making the *adhān* (call to prayer) before the commencement of the congregational prayer.

Another group of Companions who will be conferred the highest station in Paradise consists of the believers who capitalised on any opportunity to perform good deeds and serve the Prophet ﷺ. In this category, one may take into consideration the following Hadith, wherein the Prophet ﷺ said: "I saw myself entering into Jannah and immediately saw Umm Sulaym, namely the wife of Abū Ṭalḥah and the mother of Anas ibn Mālik." There are a number of reasons why this family obtained this enviable privilege in the Afterlife. For instance, Umm Sulaym ﵂ tasked her son Anas ﵁—who was a young boy at the time—with the task of serving the Prophet ﷺ and fulfilling his needs. Moreover, Abū Ṭalḥah ﵁ blessed himself and his family by giving away his garden for the sake of Allah and His Messenger ﷺ. Because of this generous act of charity, both Abū Ṭalḥah and his family will be blessed with a permanent garden in the Afterlife. In fact, this act of altruism was so great that it was indirectly praised in the following Qur'anic verse:

لَن تَنَالُواْ ٱلۡبِرَّ حَتَّىٰ تُنفِقُواْ مِمَّا تُحِبُّونَ

"You will never achieve righteousness until you donate some of what you cherish."[75]

Because of their major sacrifices and full commitment to the Prophetic call, these figures were the epitomes of the Islamic spirit. Whilst we may not be able to reach their level of devotion and loyalty, we should at the very least strive to emulate their noble example and follow their path. That way, we will be united with them in the Eternal Garden.

---

[75] *Āl 'Imrān*, 92.

21

Meeting Your Angels in Jannah

No one can dispute the fact that being surrounded by Angels is a momentous blessing, since they are pure beings who praise Allah ﷻ constantly and pray for the pious. In fact, one of the reasons why the last 10 nights of Ramadan are extraordinarily sanctified is that the presence of the Angels on Earth is increased exponentially. Moreover, when a person performs an act of good, Allah praises them in the presence of His closest Angels, who all then love him. In the Hereafter, a person's interactions with these luminescent friends of Allah will continue. For instance, the keeper of the Hellfire is an Angel named Mālik, with their name being the active participle of the Arabic word *mulk*, which refers to strength and power. This Angel will have a hideous and disfigured appearance that will horrify the inhabitants of the Hellfire. Paradise will have its own keeper, but as opposed to their counterpart Mālik, they will have a beautiful and cheerful appearance. Imams Ibn al-Qayyim and Ibn Kathīr ﷺ have related reports which indicate that the name of this Angel will be Riḍwān. Since the latter name is derived from the word *riḍā* (pleasure), this indicates that the sight of the keeper of Paradise will only further increase the contentment and rapture of the believers.

But the experience of the believers will be amplified with the presence of other Angels within the various stations and levels of Paradise. In this regard, Imam Ibn Kathīr ﷺ said: "Amongst the Angels are those who are appointed in charge of Paradise and those who are entrusted with preparing the honours for its people." In light of this statement, one deduces that there are Angels who are currently preparing the grounds of Paradise by cultivating its lands, whilst others are preparing the gifts, gardens, meals, and palaces for its inhabitants. Imam Ibn Kathīr ﷺ meticulously encapsulated this preparation process by stating: "All these Angels are anticipating the entrance of the occupants and they have prepared for us what no eye has seen, what no ear has heard, and what no mind has comprehended."

One can divide the Angels of the Afterlife into a number of formal categories. First, there will be a group of Angels whose sole function will be to issue the announcements

There are appointed angels who are currently preparing the grounds of Paradise by cultivating its lands, whilst others are preparing the gifts, gardens, meals, and palaces for its inhabitants.

promulgated by Allah ﷻ. These declarations will consist of divine statements that will be most pleasing for the people of Jannah. Another group of Angels will be simply tasked with the responsibility of congratulating the people of Jannah on a regular basis. This role has been beautifully articulated in the following Qur'anic verse, wherein Allah says:

وَالْمَلَائِكَةُ يَدْخُلُونَ عَلَيْهِم مِّن كُلِّ بَابٍ سَلَامٌ عَلَيْكُم بِمَا صَبَرْتُمْ ۚ فَنِعْمَ عُقْبَى الدَّارِ

"And the Angels will enter upon them from every gate, saying, 'Peace be upon you for your perseverance. How excellent is the ultimate abode!'"[76]

Then there will be other Angels whose role will be to exclusively serve the inhabitants of Paradise and ensure that their needs are met. Not only will they greet the occupants of Paradise recurrently and address their demands, they will provide them with any desired services, regardless of the time of day. In addition, the pleasurable experience in Jannah will be further enhanced thanks to the presence of the leading Angels, such as Mīkā'īl, Isrāfīl, and Jibrīl ﷺ, with the latter being known as Sayyid al-Malā'ikah (the Chief of the Angels). In the Qur'an, these Angels are honoured, as Allah swears by all of them:

فَالْمُقَسِّمَاتِ أَمْرًا

"...and [those Angels] administering affairs by [Allah's] command!"[77]

---

[76] *al-Ra'd*, 23–24.

[77] *al-Dhāriyāt*, 4.

Jibrīl ﷷ, who would bring down the Revelation to our beloved Prophet ﷺ in this world, is a majestic Angel who possesses more than 600 wings, with rubies and pearls falling down from each one of them. In the permanent abode of bliss, one will enjoy the opportunity to ask Jibrīl ﷷ direct and specific questions concerning the nature of revelation, the interactions he had with the Prophet ﷺ, and how Paradise was fashioned by Allah. Moreover, the senior Angel Mīkā'īl ﷷ—who is nicknamed as Malak al-Raḥmah (Angel of Mercy)—can explain to the people how he sent the winds and torrential downpours upon the people of this world with the permission of his Lord. Moreover, the inhabitants will be able to freely interact and converse with the blessed Angel Isrāfīl ﷷ. Not only does this Angel possess a beautiful voice, they will also be entrusted with the duty of blowing the Ṣūr (Trumpet) on the Day of Judgement, which will cause all the dead humans on the Earth to be revived. In Paradise, however, their role will be to entertain the Muslims with their pleasant and awesome voice. Whilst indulging in the pleasures of Paradise, the believers will also be greeted by Malak al-Mawt (The Angel of Death), who will now adopt a purely cheerful demeanour.

Whilst in Jannah, the believers will also enjoy the company of all the Angels that surrounded them and accompanied them in their worldly lives. In the temporal world, these Angels provided the believers protection from evil and harm whilst also inspiring them to perform acts of good. In the Afterlife, these Angels will further enhance the experience of Jannah with their beautiful presence and luminescence.

The evidence for their enduring presence can be found in the Qur'an, for Allah confirms that the Angels will address the believer with the following proclamation when their soul departs from this world:

نَحْنُ أَوْلِيَاؤُكُمْ فِي الْحَيَاةِ الدُّنْيَا وَفِي الْآخِرَةِ ۖ وَلَكُمْ فِيهَا مَا تَشْتَهِي أَنفُسُكُمْ وَلَكُمْ فِيهَا مَا تَدَّعُونَ

"We are your supporters in this worldly life and in the Hereafter. There you will have whatever your souls desire, and there you will have whatever you ask for."[78]

Whilst in the temporal world the believer could not see these companion Angels, they will have the capacity to perceive and address them in Paradise. In these other-worldly discussions, the Angels will recollect the special moments they shared with the believers, such as the fateful episodes where they protected them from harm or provided them a blessing owing to their supplications and prayers. The believers will be taken aback by these past episodes, as they will appreciate all the moments where Allah averted them from accidents or illnesses notwithstanding their unawareness. Other Angels will approach the believers and remind them of any special *duʿā'* (supplication) that they made in this world, which thereby caused Allah to boast of them in the heavenly court. Another group of them will cause the believers to recall the special invocations they made on Laylah al-Qadr and the special virtuous deeds

[78] *Fuṣṣilat*, 31.

they performed in the mosque and other gatherings that allowed them to earn the forgiveness of Allah. These golden points of recollection will cause the believers to rejoice and celebrate, as they will appreciate that every act of goodness was recorded and given full consideration.

ادخلوها بسلام آمنين

(It will be said to the believers)

"Enter (Jannah) in peace and security."

AL-ḤIJR, 46

In Jannah, a group of angels will remind the believers of the special duʿā's they made on Laylah al-Qadr and the many virtuous deeds they performed that allowed them to earn the forgiveness of Allah.

22

Can You Have Pets in Jannah?

Our concrete experiences in this world confirm that enjoyment and comfort are not obtained simply from inter-personal experiences, but interactions with other animals as well. This explains the phenomenon of pets, whereby we own and possess animals from a myriad of species for the purposes of entertainment and serenity. In Paradise, an extension of the latter phenomenon will endure, as Allah will create a special type of species that will enhance our level of security and peace of mind within the gardens of delight. These animals cannot be described as pets in a conventional worldly sense, since they will be heavenly beings. In one authentic Hadith, the Prophet ﷺ said: "By the One in Whose

Hand is my soul, when the believers come out of their graves, they will be received by white she-camels possessing wings and gold saddles. The laces of their hooves will be brilliantly shining, and every single step of them will be aligned to the range of vision." After assessing the bare import of this report, one may conclude that the animals gifted to the believers will be similar to the special winged mule-like creature known as the Burāq, which the Prophet ﷺ rode during his special journey of ascension known as al-Isrā' wa al-Mi'rāj. In fact, every believer will be gifted with several such riding animals. In an authentic Hadith, the Companion Abū Mas'ūd ؓ related an astonishing report: "A man brought a she-camel to the Prophet with a rope through its nose ring. And he said: 'O Messenger of Allah, I am giving this for the sake of Allah.' And the Prophet ﷺ said in response: 'On the Day of Judgement, you will have 700 she-camels—with each one of them having a rope through its nose ring—in Jannah.'" This man donated a single she-camel in charity, but on the Mīzān (Scale), it will register the reward of 700 animals. Moreover, after entering Paradise, this man will be gifted with 700 heavenly animals, which he will be able to ride in Paradise however and whenever he wishes.

However, it may naturally be the case that some individuals will prefer other animals in the place of camels. Will they enjoy the opportunity to interact and ride the animals of their choice? This question was in fact raised by a Bedouin who went to the Prophet ﷺ and said:

يَا رَسُولَ اللهِ إِنِّي أُحِبُّ الخَيْلَ، أَفِي الجَنَّةِ خَيْلٌ

"O Messenger of Allah! I am a man who loves horses. Will there be horses in Jannah?"

In response to this query, the Prophet ﷺ said:

إِنْ أُدْخِلْتَ الجَنَّةَ أُتِيتَ بِفَرَسٍ مِنْ يَاقُوتَةٍ لَهُ جَنَاحَانِ،
فَحُمِلْتَ عَلَيْهِ ثُمَّ طَارَ بِكَ حَيْثُ شِئْتَ

"If you are granted entrance into Paradise, you shall be brought a two-winged horse encrusted with rubies and then you shall be carried on it. It will take you wherever you wish."

Moreover, other majestic and exotic animals will be found in Paradise as well. For instance, there are some Hadiths which confirm that a myriad of beautiful birds—whose necks will correspond to the length of giraffes—will be found around the blessed fount of the Prophet ﷺ, which is known as al-Kawthar. These flying creatures will exceed the beauty of any fascinating birds that we have seen in this life, such as flamingos, parrots, or hummingbirds. Moreover, another Hadith states that the horizon of Paradise will be beautified with butterflies made of glittering gold, a spectacle which will dazzle the eyes of all onlookers. It is possible that these butterflies will also possess brilliant colours that no human eye has seen and no intellect has perceived in this world.

Besides the presence of tamed pets, exotic birds, and glittering insects, the inhabitants of Jannah will also be served by special heavenly servants that will be eternally youthful in their appearance. Regarding the dazzling beauty of these servants, Allah states:

وَيَطُوفُ عَلَيْهِمْ وِلْدَانٌ مُّخَلَّدُونَ إِذَا رَأَيْتَهُمْ حَسِبْتَهُمْ لُؤْلُؤًا مَّنثُورًا

"They will be waited on by eternal youths. If you saw them, you would think they were scattered pearls."[79]

Thus, these servants will be so handsome and elegant in their appearance that an onlooker would presume that they are a group of shining pearls. In fact, a number of works in the field of Qur'anic exegesis mention that when the believers enter Jannah, they will be greeted and received by 70,000 servants, with every one of them appearing like a glittering pearl. Every occupant of Paradise will be provided with the same number of servants, with all of them standing before their client and promptly responding to his needs. If the inhabitant of Paradise treks within the gardens and waterfronts of Paradise, they will be closely followed by these servants, who will ensure any of their prospective needs are met. According to Imam Ibn al-Qayyim ﷺ, Allah used the metaphor of scattered pearls to describe these servants "not simply due to their

[79] *al-Insān*, 19.

beauty and charm but also to denote their constant motion". In other words, they will not remain fixed in a given place, and instead will be constantly moving around the believers as dutiful servants.

Regarding the meticulousness of the service process in Jannah, al-Ḍaḥḥāk ﷺ narrates: "Whilst the friend of Allah is sitting in his palace in Paradise, a messenger from Allah will come to visit. This messenger—who is an Angel—will then say to the keeper: 'Seek permission for the messenger of Allah to see the friend of Allah.'" According to the narration, the messenger will then go to the occupant of Paradise and say: "O friend of Allah, here is a messenger of Allah asking permission to see you." The believer will then permit the Angel to enter. As such, the latter will appear before the believer, present a range of gifts and edibles, and then say: "O friend of Allah, Allah is sending you His *salām* and telling you to eat from this plate." Whilst the believer will be pleased with this reception, they will initially assume that they are already well-acquainted with this dish, and will subsequently say: "But I have already eaten this." The Angel will say: "No, please proceed to eat from this." The believer will comply with this demand, and upon consuming it, will experience the taste of every fruit found in Jannah. From this beautiful story, one is amazed to find that a whole line of servants will be exerting their best efforts to ensure the believer is delighted and satisfied. Such will be the case regardless of the person's level or rank. In fact, in a magnificent Hadith, Abū Hurayrah ﷺ reported that the Prophet ﷺ said: "The lowest ranked person in Jannah will have 15,000 servants in the morning and the evening. Every servant has a specific duty which their counterpart does not share." All of these services will be provided on a constant basis to ensure the occupants are pleased. But before the believers can enjoy this level of service in the Afterlife, they must exert their best efforts to serve humanity and their common brethren in this world.

ادْخُلُوهَا بِسَلَامٍ آمِنِينَ

(It will be said to the believers)

"Enter (Jannah) in peace and security."

AL-ḤIJR, 46

23

The Sounds of Jannah

In order to avoid falling into any sins or indiscretions, the believer heavily regulates their speech and only speaks when it is absolutely necessary. In a notable tradition, the Prophet ﷺ showered words of praise upon the one who attends a gathering and departs from it without being properly noticed by anyone. ʿUmar ibn al-Khaṭṭāb رضي الله عنه also once famously said that the person who speaks frequently will err frequently, and the one who errs frequently is more likely to fall into the Hellfire. In light of these reports, the believer exercises caution and observes silence to emulate the path of the Prophet ﷺ and pious predecessors. By doing so, they will be rewarded with the serenity and silence found in Paradise.

The blessed Companions of the Prophet ﷺ observed silence and restraint throughout their lives, despite facing immense persecution at the hands of the polytheists of the Quraysh. Many of them could have responded to their foes with harshness and arrogance, but instead they championed lives of humility. For instance, despite his impressive level of affluence, 'Uthmān ibn 'Affān ﵁ was an extremely modest and humble person. Moreover, despite having an unparalleled rank in beauty, lineage, and affluence, the Mother of the Believers Khadījah ﵂ always displayed the uppermost degree of modesty and humbleness in her interactions. Because of her tranquil disposition, she will be rewarded with a home in Paradise that will confer her the highest level of serenity and repose-fulness. The word that is used in the Qur'an to demonstrate this unparalleled type of peacefulness in Jannah is known as *naṣab*, and it will be unlike any degree of quietude found in this world. Such a conclusion can be inferred from the following Qur'anic verse:

الَّذِي أَحَلَّنَا دَارَ الْمُقَامَةِ مِن فَضْلِهِ لَا يَمَسُّنَا فِيهَا نَصَبٌ وَلَا يَمَسُّنَا فِيهَا لُغُوبٌ

"[He is the One] Who—out of His grace—has settled us in the Home of Everlasting Stay, where we will be touched by neither fatigue nor weariness."[80]

80 *Fāṭir*, 35.

The hymns and songs of praise recited by the Angels in Jannah will supersede the sound of any tune or melody found in this world. Besides the birds and Angels, Allah will command Prophet Dāwūd عليه السلام to glorify Him with a beautiful and soothing voice.

This handsome reward will be conferred to them as a result of their beautiful patience, for they endured years of persecution and harm at the hands of the polytheists of Mecca without any complaints or grievances. Indeed, these Companions were perfect examples of the *ʿibād al-Raḥmān* (servants of the Most Merciful), whereby they would respond to harm with the message of peace. Muslims of later eras must strive to emulate their standards by refraining from spiteful speech and avoiding any gatherings where a person is slandered or denigrated. By doing so, they will be able to maintain the inherent purity of their *fiṭrah* (natural disposition), which innately dislikes indulging in such affairs. Because they observed silence in these affairs and refrained from idle speech, Allah will reward them with eternals gardens in the Afterlife that will be free of any disturbances and commotions. Regarding the tranquil state that will be found in Jannah, Allah states:

لَّا تَسۡمَعُ فِيهَا لَٰغِيَةٗ

"[Therein] no idle talk will be heard."[81]

Another verse of the Qur'an specifically outlines the individuals who will receive this reward:

ٱلَّذِينَ هُمۡ عَنِ ٱللَّغۡوِ مُعۡرِضُونَ

"[Successful are] those who avoid idle talk."[82]

---

[81] *al-Ghāshiyah*, 11.

[82] *al-Mu'minūn*, 3.

Thus, the ones who safeguard themselves from vain speech in this world will be protected from it in the Afterlife. Once they enter the gardens of Paradise, they will receive the greeting of peace from every Angel or fellow believer that passes by them. Regarding these beautiful interactions, Allah states the following in the Qur'an:

لَا يَسْمَعُونَ فِيهَا لَغْوًا إِلَّا سَلَامًا

"There they will never hear any idle talk—
only [greetings of] peace."[83]

This is why our beloved Prophet ﷺ said:

أَيُّهَا النَّاسَ أَفْشُوا السَّلَامَ وَأَطْعِمُوا الطَّعَامَ وَصَلُّوا بِاللَّيْلِ
وَالنَّاسُ نِيَامٌ تَدْخُلُوا الجَنَّةَ بِسَلَامٍ

"O people! Spread the salām (greeting of peace), provide food (to the needy), pray in the night whilst others are sleeping, and you will enter Paradise in peace."

This is why in the sacred Islamic tradition, Paradise is conferred the eminent title of Dār al-Salām (The Abode of Peace). In fact, one of the sacred names of Allah is al-Salām, which signifies how He is the source of peace itself. In Paradise, this theme of peace will be actualized to the highest degree imaginable, as the Creator and His Angels will approach the inhabitants of Paradise and issue their respective greetings:

---

83 *Maryam*, 62.

تَحِيَّتُهُمْ يَوْمَ يَلْقَوْنَهُۥ سَلَٰمٌ

"Their greeting on the Day they meet Him will be, 'Peace!'"[84]

In the temporal world, it is often the case that people visit a park or other natural setting to dispel their worries and relieve their anxieties in their life; individuals desire such a state of solitude to be temporarily freed of their psychological pain or social troubles. When observed externally, such individuals appear cheerful and satisfied, but in reality, their inner disposition is submerged in a wave of perplexities. But once they enter Jannah, the trips that the believers will undertake in the heavenly gardens and water fronts will be without any such worries. Both their internal and external conditions will be free of the slightest element of disquiet. Allah states the following concerning the occupants of Paradise:

أَلَا إِنَّ أَوْلِيَاءَ اللَّهِ لَا خَوْفٌ عَلَيْهِمْ وَلَا هُمْ يَحْزَنُونَ

"There will certainly be no fear for the close servants of Allah, nor will they grieve."[85]

In fact, the believers will be so pleased and content in Paradise that they will glorify Allah's name by saying:

الْحَمْدُ لِلَّهِ الَّذِىٓ أَذْهَبَ عَنَّا الْحَزَنَ

"And they will say, 'Praise be to Allah, Who has kept away from us all sorrow.'"[86]

---

84 *al-Aḥzāb*, 44.

85 *Yūnus*, 62.

86 *Fāṭir*, 34.

Besides the wonderful sights and delights in Paradise, it is important to note that the permanent abode of bliss will entertain the believers with the most pleasant of melodies. In this regard, Saʿd ibn Saʿīd al-Ḥārithī ﷺ said: "There are forests of golden bamboo in Jannah that are loaded with pearls. And when the people of Jannah desire to hear a beautiful sound, Allah will send a wind that will bring about whatever sound that they desire." From this report, one deduces that the wind will be empowered with the ability to play musical notes and tunes that will delight all listeners. The believers will be rewarded with these beautiful melodies due to their commitment to the divine law of Allah by not listening to the corrupt music of this world. In a report narrated by Muhammad ibn al-Munkadir ﷺ, the believers will be rewarded in the following manner: "On the Day of Judgement, a caller will proclaim: 'Where are those who protected their ears and themselves from the meetings of amusement and the instruments of Shayṭān? Put them on the dunes of musk.'" Then Allah will say:

أَسْمِعُوهُمْ تَمْجِيدِي وَتَحْمِيدِي

"Make them hear My glorification and My praise."

The hymns and songs of praise recited by the Angels will supersede the sound of any tune or melody found in this world. The reason why this is the case is latently expressed in a narration reported by Shahr ibn Ḥawshab ﷺ: "Allah will say to the Angels: 'My devoted slaves loved beautiful voices in this world, but they abandoned some of them for My sake.

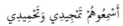

So, make them hear what is even more beautiful.'" Thus, the one who avoids listening to that which is sinful in this world will be handsomely recompensed with the lovely ballads of the Angels. Some facts have been transmitted concerning the melodic nature of some of these Angels. For instance, Imam al-Awzāʿī ﵀ said: "There is no one who has a more beautiful voice amongst the creation of Allah than Isrāfīl." Originally entrusted with the task of blowing the Trumpet on the Day of Judgement, Isrāfīl's role in Paradise will be to entertain the believers with his awesome and soothing voice.

Besides the birds and Angels, there will also be a Prophet who will recite beautiful hymns within Paradise as well. That Prophet will be none other than Dāwūd ﵇, who is known for his melodious voice. In one notable Qur'anic verse, Allah states:

وَإِنَّ لَهُۥ عِندَنَا لَزُلْفَىٰ وَحُسْنَ مَـَٔابٍ

"And he will indeed have [a status of] closeness to Us and an honourable destination!"[87]

[87] *Ṣād*, 40.

Mālik ibn Dīnār commented on this verse by stating: "When the Day of Judgement occurs, a high pulpit will be placed in Jannah and Allah will say: 'O Dāwūd, glorify Me with that beautiful and soothing voice which you used to glorify Me with in the world.' And Dāwūd will start to glorify Allah, and that will capture the attention of the people of Jannah and give them joy." May Allah grant us all entrance to the permanent abode of bliss, so we may listen to these beautiful hymns and sing along with them as well for all of eternity.

ادْخُلُوهَا بِسَلَامٍ آمِنِينَ

(It will be said to the believers)

"Enter (Jannah) in peace and security."

AL-ḤIJR, 46

When the people of Jannah desire to hear a beautiful sound, Allah will send a wind that will bring about whatever sound that they desire. The believers will be rewarded with these beautiful melodies due to their commitment to the divine law of Allah by not listening to the corrupt music of this world.

24

Dhikr in Jannah

Whether it is experiencing a car accident, facing the loss of a loved one, or committing a sin, the immediate reaction to a major lifetime event is a pivotal moment. How one reacts is determinative of their level of faith and their ability to orient their deeds and mindset towards Allah. After all, the Prophet ﷺ said:

إِنَّمَا الصَّبْرُ عِندَ الصَّدمَةِ الأُولَى

"Patience is only at the very first strike."

If a Muslim reacts to a tragedy by resisting the evil urges of Shayṭān, praising Allah, and remembering their inevitable return to Him, they will raise their status and become from one of His close servants. Such an illustration of patience and deference to Allah's will is more valuable than anything found in this world.

إِنَّ الَّذِينَ اتَّقَوْا إِذَا مَسَّهُمْ طَٰٓئِفٌ مِّنَ الشَّيْطَٰنِ تَذَكَّرُوا فَإِذَا هُم مُّبْصِرُونَ

"Indeed, when Satan whispers to those mindful, they remember [Allah] and then they start to see clearly."[88]

To be successful in the Afterlife, a Muslim must be in constant remembrance of Allah in this temporal world. Should they experience a pleasant event, they should immediately recite the invocation of *alḥamdulillāh* (all praise is due to Allah). If they fall into a sin, they should turn to Allah's repentance and say the formula *astaghfirullāh* (I seek the forgiveness of Allah). And lastly, they should be able to utter the declaration of faith at the point of death by saying *lā ilāha illa Allāh* (there is no God but Allah), for that will allow them to enter Paradise with ease. In Paradise, this blessed cycle of *dhikr* (remembrance of the divine) will continue, as a person will be surrounded by Angels and the Prophets who will be constantly glorifying Allah. But even more importantly, a person will be able to witness the rewards and dividends for every single litany or word of divine praise that they uttered in this world: because of their frequent recitation of formulas of *dhikr,* they will find castles, trees, and gardens built in their name. One should never underestimate the value of

88 *al-A'rāf,* 201.

In Paradise, our love for Allah will be so great that we will constantly observe the remembrance of His blessed name. The observance of dhikr will not be one of the obligations in Jannah, but instead, it will be performed to gain constant pleasure and enjoyment.

these litanies. As noted in a previous chapter, a single unit of *tasbīḥ* (glorification of Allah) exceeds the value of the entire kingdom of Sulaymān ﷺ. Moreover, in an authentic tradition, the Prophet ﷺ said: "The invocation *lā ḥawla wa lā quwwata illā bi Allāh* (there is no might nor power except with Allah) is one of the treasures of Paradise." In another report, he said that this expression is written under the Throne of Allah. Similarly, Ṣafwān ibn Sulaym ﷺ is reported to have said: "No Angel has risen from the Earth until they said *lā ḥawla wa lā quwwata illā bi Allāh.*" To encourage the regular recital of this supplication, a Hadith prescribes putting one's trust in Allah and saying *lā ḥawla wa lā quwwata illā bi Allāh* every time they exit their house. These supplications consist of a few simple words that are extremely easy to recite, so every time a person fails to recite them, a reward in the Afterlife is lost. This is why Imam Ibn al-Jawzī ﷺ said:

فَأَسْرِعْ بِأَخَفِّ مَا خَفَّ وَزْنُه قَلَّ ثَمَنُه

"So, hasten towards performing those acts that are lightweight but of heavy value."

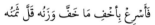

Through this statement, this great Imam is reminding us that words of *dhikr* require only a few seconds to recite, yet they accrue eternal rewards. In essence, through these simple formulas Allah is providing His servants the opportunity to construct permanent houses in Paradise, with such an arrangement being the best bargain imaginable. One should then ensure that they spend a portion of their day articulating the *tahlīl* (declaring the oneness of Allah) and *taḥmīd*

(praising of Allah) of their Creator. They should also partake in *istighfār* (seeking forgiveness) and recite numerous rounds of *ṣalawāt* (prayers) upon the Messenger of Allah ﷺ on a regular basis.

The Prophetic Sunnah confirms that whilst regular acts of worship—such as prayer—will cease in Jannah, all formulas of *dhikr* will continue to exist. In an authentic Hadith, the Prophet ﷺ is reported to have said: "The people of Paradise will eat and drink, but they will not blow their noses or relieve themselves. Their food will be digested through the mechanism of burping and sweating, which will emit the fragrance of musk. And they will be inspired to partake in the *tasbīḥ* and *taḥmīd* the way that you all naturally breathe." In another report, the Prophet ﷺ added: "They will glorify Allah in the morning and evening." Thus, the people of Paradise will be naturally predisposed to recite words of *dhikr* in all times and circumstances, as the magnificent creatures and structures around them will enrapture them and stir them to remember Allah. These aforementioned facts should be no surprise, since the inhabitants of Paradise were the people of *dhikr* during their time in this temporal world, which explains why they will be so inclined to remember Allah in the Afterlife as well. In an authentic Hadith, the Prophet ﷺ said: "The people of *dhikr* will be the first to enter Paradise." In another report, he specifically described them to be from the *Ḥammādūn* (the ones who constantly praise Allah). Such people are the opposite of the *Jahannamiyūn* (the former inhabitants of the Hellfire), who will have to enter Jannah last due to their negligence in remembering Allah during their time in this world. Thus, there is a strong correlation between the level of dhikr one makes and how early they will be granted admission into Jannah.

Imam al-Qurṭubī ﷺ is reported to have said: "This *tasbīḥ* made in Jannah will not be an obligation or imposed upon you. The matter is just as Jābir described: 'They will be inspired with *tasbīḥ* and *takbīr* just as they breathe.'" To further illustrate this fascinating phenomenon, al-Qurṭubī mentioned that the *dhikr* of Allah will in many respects assume the act of breathing. In other words, just as we breathe in the world without any conscious effort on our part, in the Afterlife we will praise and glorify Allah's name without the need for any active intention on our part. In Paradise, our love for Allah will be so great that we will constantly observe the remembrance of His name. For this reason, Imam Ibn Taymiyyah ﷺ said: "This observance of *tasbīḥ* and *takbīr* is one of the pleasures of the people of Paradise. It will not be one of the obligations or deeds that are performed for the attainment of a specific reward. Instead, it will be performed in Paradise to gain pleasure and enjoyment."

Whenever a person recites the phrase *alḥamdulillāh*, they do so for a specific reason. For instance, after finishing a meal, a person is recommended to say:

الْحَمْدُ لِلَّهِ الَّذِي أَطْعَمَنِي هٰذَا

"All praise be to Allah Who fed me this."

Likewise, after a person puts on their clothing, they should say:

الْحَمْدُ لِلَّهِ الَّذِي أَلْبَسَنِي هٰذَا الثَّوْب

"All praise be to Allah Who clothed me with this garment."

Thus, in all episodes where Allah is praised in this world, there is an underlying cause associated with them, regardless of whether they are explicit or latent. It is interesting to note that in the Afterlife, the believers will be praising Allah as well. But on this occasion, the causal factor will be completely different. In the Qur'an, we find that after being admitted into Paradise, some of the believers will praise Allah by saying:

الْحَمْدُ لِلَّهِ الَّذِي أَذْهَبَ عَنَّا الْحَزَنَ

"Praise be to Allah, Who has kept away from us all sorrow."[89]

The beauty of this supplication should not be overlooked, for it marks the believers celebrating how all forms of sadness, trauma, and anxiety will disappear once and for all.

[89] *Fāṭir*, 34.

After reflecting on their salvation and the pleasures that lie within the plane of Paradise, the believers will come to the realisation that they could only obtain these delights through the grace of Allah alone:

الْحَمْدُ لِلَّهِ الَّذِي هَدَانَا لِهَٰذَا وَمَا كُنَّا لِنَهْتَدِيَ لَوْلَا أَنْ هَدَانَا اللَّهُ

"Praise be to Allah for guiding us to this. We would have never been guided if Allah had not guided us."[90]

The believers will then recall the critical moments of their respective lifetimes and the various crises of faith they had to endure. They will thank Allah for His divine protection, for without it, they would have likely succumbed to their desires and strayed from the straight path:

الْحَمْدُ لِلَّهِ الَّذِي صَدَقَنَا وَعْدَهُ وَأَوْرَثَنَا الْأَرْضَ نَتَبَوَّأُ مِنَ الْجَنَّةِ حَيْثُ نَشَاءُ

"Praise be to Allah Who has fulfilled His promise to us, and made us inherit the land to settle in Paradise wherever we please."[91]

Likewise, the members of the Jahannamiyūn who exit the Hellfire will thank and praise Allah for His deliverance. In sum, all the believers in Paradise—regardless of whether they entered there immediately or after enduring a degree of punishment in the Hellfire—will sing the praises of their Lord. And the beauty of this scenery will be further amplified as the inhabitants of Paradise will be smiling towards one another and issuing the *salām* (greeting of peace).

---

90 *al-Aʿrāf*, 43.

91 *Zumar*, 74.

25

Your Inheritance in Jannah

One of the most inspirational quotations coined in recent history is the following maxim: "Goal minus doubt equals reality." In other words, if a person truly aims to achieve an overarching end in life and has faith in their capacities, they will overcome all odds and eventually succeed. Whilst it is unfortunate to find that many individuals use this motto as a means to achieve materialistic goals in this temporal world, Muslims can operationalise it as a formula for success in the Hereafter. This otherworldly perspective can only be activated if one orients themselves towards the Hereafter and frees themselves from the trappings of the materialism found in this world. There is a beautiful story regarding the Prophet ﷺ which effectively encapsulates this concept. In this notable incident, 'Umar ibn al-Khaṭṭāb ﷺ once entered the room of the Prophet ﷺ, and was shocked to find how desolate and impoverished it was; in it, he could see a rough makeshift mattress that was made of tree branches, whilst a pillow-like top piece was made of palm fibres. 'Umar ﷺ noticed that this bed case was so primitive and rough that it had marred the back of the Prophet ﷺ with a number of bruises and marks. Such a sight caused 'Umar ﷺ to cry, for he could not fathom that the best of creation was relegated to such a constricted state. The Prophet ﷺ noticed 'Umar's emotional state, and said: "Why are you crying, O 'Umar?" 'Umar ﷺ said in response: "O Messenger of Allah, I have seen the palaces of Kisrā (Chosroes) in Persia and the palaces of Qayṣar (Caesar) in Rome, and you deserve far more than all that!" The Prophet ﷺ then said: "Are you in doubt, O 'Umar? Are you not pleased that they have this world and we have the Hereafter?" From this narration, one infers that the temporal world is nothing more than an illusion that only provides limited happiness. The wise believing person does not succumb to these vain pleasures, and instead remembers the words of the Prophet ﷺ: "The temporal world is a prison for the believer and a paradise for the disbeliever." Thus, in light of this report, the believer should regulate their conduct and ensure that they merely view this world as a means to their ultimate destination: Paradise.

A Hadith states that when a believer dies and enters their grave, not only will they be presented with a striking image of their place in Paradise, they will also be shown the place they would have occupied in the Hellfire had they lived an immoral lifestyle. In the case of the disbelievers, the converse is true: not only will they be shown their place in Hell, but they will also be shown the spot in Paradise they would have resided in had they accepted Allah and His message. This report implicitly lends credence to a powerful concept championed by some scholars, namely that the believers will not only inhabit their own appointed locations in Paradise, but they will also be granted the spots in Paradise that the disbelievers failed to earn through their deeds in this life.

In one important passage of the Qur'an, Allah states:

أُولَٰٓئِكَ هُمُ الْوَٰرِثُونَ الَّذِينَ يَرِثُونَ الْفِرْدَوْسَ هُمْ فِيهَا خَٰلِدُونَ

"These are the ones who will inherit Paradise as their own. They will be there forever."[92]

The exegetes of the Qur'an disagree on what the term inheritance mentioned in this verse denotes. One group of scholars argued that this verse indicates how the believers will obtain Paradise in an effortless manner, just as a person receives the rightful share of their inheritance. However, another set of commentators posit that this verse is explained by a Prophetic Hadith which states: "There is not any one of you who lives in this life except that they have two positions: a home in the Hellfire and a home in Paradise."

[92] *al-Mu'minūn*, 10–11.

As a reward for all the sacrifices and devotion to the truth, the believers will not only be given their spots of Paradise that bear their respective names, but they will also inherit the gardens, palaces, and residences that were tentatively appointed for the disbelievers as well.

The same report then states that once a person assumes their spot in Paradise, their location in the Hellfire will be destroyed. As for the people who enter the Hellfire, their places in Paradise will be left intact and given to the entrants of Paradise. As such, the believers will not simply be given the spots of Paradise that bear their respective names, but they will also inherit the gardens, palaces, and residences that were tentatively appointed for the disbelievers as well. This will be a just recompense, since unlike the rejectors of the truth, the believers made many sacrifices in this world and abstained from many pleasures. Regarding the possessions that the believers will inherit from the non-Muslims, Saʿīd ibn Jubayr ﵀ notes that the transfer is not merely due to the disbelief of the wrongdoers, but also their failure to pray, pay *zakāh*, and fast—the number of rewards that would have been allotted to them if such actions were executed will be counted and deposited in the accounts of the believers instead.

However, this aforementioned discussion naturally yields an important question: do the believers earn entry into Paradise due to their good deeds? This *prima facie* appears to be the case in light of the following Qur'anic verse:

وَتِلْكَ الْجَنَّةُ الَّتِي أُورِثْتُمُوهَا بِمَا كُنْتُمْ تَعْمَلُونَ

"That is the Paradise which you will be awarded for what you used to do."[93]

[93] *al-Zukhruf*, 72.

However, the exegetes and commentators state that the sequence "for what you used to do" should be read figuratively. In actual fact, all of the believers will enter Paradise solely due to the mercy of Allah, not as a result of their virtuous deeds. However, Allah and His Angels will inform us that deeds were the decisive factor in attaining salvation in order to imbue a sense of accomplishment and merit. At a basic level, human psychology functions according to the lens of compensation and remuneration. Such expressions will not only be fundamental in amplifying the experience of believers in Paradise, they also propel the righteous individuals in this world to lead lives of virtue and morality.

ادْخُلُوهَا بِسَلَامٍ آمِنِينَ

(It will be said to the believers)

"Enter (Jannah) in peace and security."

AL-ḤIJR, 46

26

The Highest Level of Jannah

It is narrated that 'Umar ibn al-Khaṭṭāb رضي الله عنه once said: "If there were to be a caller from the Heavens who said that everyone will be going to Paradise except for one person, I would fear that I am that very person." 'Umar رضي الله عنه then continued by stating: "And if there were to be a caller who said that every person will go to Hellfire except for one person, then I would be hopeful that I am that very person." Such a marvellous statement from this eminent Companion demonstrates how the early predecessors of this religion had hope in Allah's mercy whilst also fearing His eternal punishment. A Muslim should emulate these values and aspire to attain the best rewards and possessions in the Afterlife.

As such, they should ask Allah for al-Firdaws—the highest plane of Paradise—and ensure their deeds and actions are most pleasing to Him.

Most interestingly, Jannah consists of a myriad of levels and planes, with each one of them reflecting a particular theme or value. One of the highest stations is known as al-Ma'wā, regarding which Ka'b ﷺ is reported to have said: "This is the domain of the *shuhadā'* (martyrs), who will assume the form of green birds. There they will be waiting for al-Raḥmān (the Possessor of Mercy) to bring them into the ultimate plane of Jannah." This account thus leads one to conclude that al-Ma'wā will be a station of relief for the individuals who died in the path of Allah.

Another plane of Jannah is known as Jannāt al-'Adn, which can be translated as the Garden of Eden. However, this station itself will actually consist of a number of levels, with every one of them containing luscious and colourful gardens. It is reported that 'Abdullāh ibn 'Umar ﷺ said: "Allah created four things with His Hand: the Throne, the Pen, al-'Adn, and Adam. As for the rest of the creation, He said, 'Be!' and it was." This narration confirms that al-'Adn has been crafted in a specific fashion that exceeds the quality of all other dimensions of the world. In this regard, it is also reported that the Prophet ﷺ said: "Allah created Jannāt al-'Adn with His Hand, putting one brick of white pearl, another one made of red rubies, and yet another consisting of green crystal. Its floor is made of musk, its ground consists of pearls, and its grasses are fashioned with saffron. Allah then ordered it to speak, and it said in reply:

قَدْ اَفْلَحَ الْمُؤْمِنُوْنَ

'Successful indeed are the believers.'"[94]

The Prophet ﷺ then noted that Allah said in reply:

وَعِزَّتِي، وَجَلَالِي لَا يُجَاوِرُنِي فِيكِ بَخِيلٌ

"I swear by My Majesty and Honour, no stingy person is going to be My neighbour in you."

This divine declaration from Allah indicates that the reward of generosity embedded within Jannāt al-'Adn will only be allotted to generous people. To illustrate this point, the Prophet ﷺ recited the following verse:

وَ مَنْ يُّوْقَ شُحَّ نَفْسِهٖ فَاُولٰٓئِكَ هُمُ الْمُفْلِحُوْنَ

"And whoever is saved from the selfishness of their own souls, it is they who are successful."[95]

Besides being generous in one's interpersonal interactions, it is necessary for one to lead a pious life, such that they will be considered from the *awliyā'* (friends of the Divine). This can be appreciated by noting the narrations that have been transmitted concerning al-Firdaws, which constitutes the highest level of

94 *al-Mu'minūn*, 1.

95 *al-Ḥashr*, 9.

Jannāt al-'Adn. In this regard, Shimr ibn 'Aṭiyyah ﵀ relates the following report: "Allah created al-Firdaws with His Hand and He has it opened five times every day. On every occasion, he addresses it by saying:

اِزْدَادِي حُسْنًا وَطِيبًا لِأَوْلِيَائِي

"Increase in goodness and beauty for My friends."

Moreover, in a beautiful tradition, the Prophet ﷺ said: "When you ask Allah, do not simply ask Him for Jannah. Rather, ask Him for al-Firdaws. It is the best and highest plane of Jannah, and above it is the Throne of al-Raḥmān. And from it flow the rivers of Jannah." This report should inspire every person to embody the virtuous characteristics required for attaining al-Firdaws, as well as avoiding any qualities that cause one to be disqualified from entering it. Regarding the latter attributes, the Messenger of Allah ﷺ said: "When Allah created al-Firdaws by His Hand, he forbade it for every *mushrik* (polytheist) as well as those addicted to wine and intoxicants." Whilst the inclusion of shirk (polytheism) as a disqualifying factor is self-evident, the invocation of wine requires some reflection. It draws to our attention the fact that no person can expect the highest plane of Paradise if they constantly indulge in the lowliest of sins; a person cannot reasonably claim that they seek al-Firdaws if they are constantly consuming *al-khabā'ith* (filthy substances) whilst also lacking the determination to improve their conduct.

Another high station of Paradise is known as al-Wasīlah, which can only be reserved for one person. In a notable Hadith, the Prophet ﷺ said:

إِنَّ الوَسِيلَةَ دَرَجَةٌ عِنْدَ اللهِ تَعَالَى لَيْسَ فَوْقَهَا دَرَجَةٌ، فَسَلُوا اللهَ تَعَالَى أَنْ يُؤْتِيَنِي الوَسِيلَةَ

"Al-Wasīlah is a degree in the sight of Allah, and there is no other degree which exceeds it. So, ask Allah to grant me al-Wasīlah."

One notes that in this report, the Prophet ﷺ is actually requesting his ummah to make *du'ā'* to Allah that he be granted al-Wasīlah. The rationale behind this request can be appreciated by the fact that it is directly connected to the Throne of Allah, and represents the apex point of the cosmos. Regarding the special qualities of this station, Ibn al-Qayyim ؒ said: "It is a place perched out for one person in the highest place of Jannah." Quite intuitively, this special station should be allotted to the best member of humankind, namely a person who can intercede on behalf of the entire Muslim nation on the Day of Judgement. This person is none other than the Messenger of Allah ﷺ, who as the last Prophet of the Universe possesses the strongest and most intimate connection with Allah. No individual in human history guided more people to the path of Paradise than him, and as such he is worthy of being the chief intercessor on the Day of Judgement. The Prophet ﷺ advised his nation to ask Allah to grant him this rank by stating: "When you hear the *mu'adhdhin* (caller) make the *adhān* (call to prayer), then send *ṣalawāt* (blessings) upon me. For every time you send *ṣalawāt* upon me, Allah will send ten blessings upon you. And then ask

Allah to grant me al-Wasīlah, which is a status in Paradise that only one servant of Allah will attain. I hope that I shall be that person. And whoever asks al-Wasīlah for me, then my *shafāʿah* (intercession) will be due for that person." The Prophet ﷺ instructed his followers to recite the following *duʿā'* to ensure he becomes the recipient of this lofty station:

اللَّهُمَّ رَبَّ هَذِهِ الدَّعْوَةِ التَّامَّةِ وَالصَّلَاةِ القَائِمَةِ آتِ مُحَمَّدًا الوَسِيلَةَ وَالفَضِيلَةَ
وَابْعَثْهُ مَقَامًا مَحْمُودًا الَّذِي وَعَدْتَهُ إِنَّكَ لَا تُخْلِفُ المِيعَادَ

"O Allah, Lord of this perfect call and established prayer, grant Muhammad al-Wasīlah and lofty rewards and give him the honoured station that You have promised him. Surely, You do not neglect Your promise."

Once empowered with the rank of al-Wasīlah, the Prophet ﷺ will invoke this station to grant the members of his ummah *wasā'il* (connections), whereby they will have their sins forgiven and be granted into Paradise. The Prophet ﷺ gave his nation glad tidings of Paradise, for after mentioning al-Wasīlah, he instructed his followers to ask Allah for al-Firdaws. Once the believers are granted entry into Paradise, they will enjoy the greatest blessing possible: being united with the Messenger of Allah himself. It is reported that al-Qaʿqāʿ al-Awsī ﷺ was once asked: "Inform of us something that will cause us to desire Jannah with eagerness." In response, he said:

فِيهَا رَسُولُ اللهِ

"In it is the Messenger of Allah."

27

Seeing Allah in Jannah

In order to love Allah and attain His grace and favour, one must strive to learn His majestic Names and Attributes. The appreciation of His holy titles will inspire one to follow His ordinances, avoid everything He has prohibited, and even partake in supererogatory deeds. Whilst emulation of the divine commandments will allow one to attain proximity to Allah in this world, true felicity will be found in the Hereafter when Allah will reveal His noble Face. Muslim theologians and jurists concur that there will be no pleasure greater in the Hereafter than being called by Allah and being granted the opportunity to see Him. It is His beauty and sublimity which causes Paradise to be radiant and brimming with light.

His sight will enthral the believers with the uppermost degree of happiness and pleasure, for they will know that their Creator is pleased with them. The Prophet ﷺ is reported to have said: "Indeed the lowest-ranked person in Paradise will observe his gardens, spouses, bounties, servants, and beds for a thousand years. And the highest ranked person and most noble one with Allah is the one who will look at the Face of Allah every morning and evening." Then the Prophet ﷺ recited the following verse:

وُجُوهٌ يَوْمَئِذٍ نَّاضِرَةٌ إِلَىٰ رَبِّهَا نَاظِرَةٌ

"On that Day faces will be bright, looking at their Lord."[96]

Another Qur'anic verse confirms that the bounties of Paradise will be so great that they will cause the faces of the believers to brim with happiness:

تَعْرِفُ فِي وُجُوهِهِمْ نَضْرَةَ النَّعِيمِ

"You will recognise on their faces the glow of delight."[97]

This joy will be a product of the realisation that every good deed performed in the temporal world yielded a particular reward, such as a castle, river, or tree. But the greatest pleasure will undoubtedly be the Beatific Vision, whereby one will be able to view Allah without any barriers. Such a privilege will be allotted to the people of *iḥsān* (religious excellence); since they worshipped Allah and paid heed to

---

96 *al-Qiyāmah*, 22–23.

97 *al-Muṭaffifīn*, 24.

There will be no greater pleasure in the Hereafter than the opportunity to see Allah. It is His beauty and sublimity that causes Paradise to be radiant and brimming with light. His sight will enthral the believers with the uppermost degree of happiness and pleasure.

His commands as if they could see Him, in the Afterlife they will be granted the gift of seeing Him directly. Because they worshipped Allah throughout the day and night in the temporal world, they will see Allah throughout the day and night in Paradise. On one occasion, a Companion asked the Prophet ﷺ: "O Messenger of Allah, will every person have the ability to see Allah in Jannah?" In response, the Prophet ﷺ said: "You shall certainly see your Lord just as you see the full Moon at the darkest point of the night. And you will not have to crowd against one another in order to see Him." As such, every person will be able to see Allah without the slightest degree of difficulty or ambiguity. There are some reports which suggest that all the believers will be provided the opportunity to see Allah on the day of Friday. The nature of this visual perception of the Divine has been elaborately explained in another Hadith: "Your Lord has singled out a valley in Paradise which has hills of white musk. And on Friday, Allah, in all of His Majesty, will address the people of Jannah from His Throne." The Hadith then mentions how the Prophets 𑁍 will be provided seats of light, whilst others will be provided pulpits of light and gold that are encrusted with gems. The pulpits will be provided for the *ṣiddīqūn* (champion of the truth) and the *shuhadā'* (martyrs). Then the eminent people of the *ghuraf* (special rooms) will exit their special suites and sit on the special hills provided for them. Allah will then address all the believers by stating:

هٰذَا يَوْم المَزِيْدِ

"This is the day of increase."

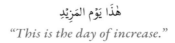

This divine proclamation is an allusion to the following Qur'anic verse:

لَهُم مَّا يَشَاءُونَ فِيهَا وَلَدَيْنَا مَزِيدٌ

"There they will have whatever they desire, and with Us is more."[98]

A number of exegetes have mentioned that the expression "and with Us is more" is a reference to seeing the Face of Allah. Many exegetical authorities have argued that a similar allusion can be found in another passage of the Qur'an:

لِلَّذِينَ أَحْسَنُوا الْحُسْنَىٰ وَزِيَادَةٌ

"Those who do good will have the finest reward and more."[99]

The Companions ﷺ found this verse fascinating, since in their view, the allotment of "the finest reward" should *prima facie* be deemed sufficient by the entrant of Paradise. They wondered what more could be offered to the believers in the abode of bliss. The Prophet ﷺ addressed their curiosity by elucidating the intended meaning of the "and more" portion of the verse:

النَّظَرُ إِلَى وَجْهِهِ الكَرِيمِ

"To gaze at the noble Face of Allah."

---

98 *Qāf*, 35.
99 *Yūnus*, 26.

The exact mechanics and dynamics of this wonderful process are elucidated in a beautiful Hadith Qudsī. Whilst they are indulging in the pleasures of Paradise, the believers will be summoned by a caller who will inform them Allah is welcoming visitors. In response, the believers will say: "We hear and obey." They will set out towards a valley, which will have an erected platform containing seats made of gold, silver, pearls, and other gems. The Prophet ﷺ mentioned that the lowest-ranked believers amongst them will be provided "a sheet made of pearls, yet every party will assume that they have the best seat in the house". As they are seated, a caller will shout: "O people of Paradise, you now have an appointment with Allah. His Majesty intends to fulfil your reward." The people of Paradise will be somewhat baffled by this statement, and will consequently ask: "What is it?" The statement of the caller will appear rather bizarre for them at first sight, since in their mind all the pleasures already allotted to them within Paradise are sufficient. But in the midst of this murmuring, a vivid light will be emitted that will cause all the planes of Jannah to be illuminated. The people of Paradise will find the divine radiance of Allah before them, a sight which will fill their hearts and minds with delight. Allah will then say to them:

يَا أَهْلَ الْجَنَّةِ سَلَامٌ عَلَيْكُمْ

"O people of Paradise, peace be upon you."

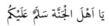

The inhabitants of Jannah will respond with the following supplication:

اللَّهُمَّ أنتَ السَّلاَمُ وَمِنْكَ السَّلاَمُ، تَبَارَكْتَ يَا ذَا الجَلاَلِ وَالإِكْرَامِ

"O Allah, You are Peace and peace comes from You. How blessed are You, O Possessor of Glory and Honour!"

Allah will then reveal Himself before the people of Jannah and then ask:

اَيْنَ عِبَادِي الَّذِيْنَ اَطَاعُوْنِي بِالْغَيْبِ وَلَمْ يَرَوْنِي هٰذَا يَوْم المَزِيْدِ فَاسْئَلُوْنِي

"Where are My servants who used to worship Me even though they could not see Me? This is the Day of Increase, so ask Me whatever you wish."

The people of Paradise will collectively respond: "We are pleased, O Allah, so be pleased with us." Allah will then say: "O people of Paradise, if I was not pleased with you, I would not have allowed you to dwell within My Garden." Then He will pose the same question once more:

هٰذَا يَوْم مَّزِيْد فَاسْئَلُوْنِي

"This is the day of increase, so ask Me whatever you wish."

The people of Paradise will convene for short group discussion amongst themselves, and then will reply to their Creator by stating:

أَرِنَا وَجْهَكَ نَنْظُرْ إِلَيهِ

"Show us Your face, so that we may see it."

Allah will then positively respond to their command. The beauty of His face will enthral them to the extent that they will completely forget the minutest amount of pain or discomfort that they experienced during their time in the temporal world. Then every person will be granted the opportunity to have a private conversation with their Lord, whereby He will remind them of their private sins and how He forgave them without holding them to account. The Beatific Vision and the opportunity to speak directly with Allah are undoubtedly the greatest experiences in Jannah. This explains why the Prophet ﷺ would often make the following supplication:

اَللّٰهُمَّ نَسْأَلُكَ لَذَّةَ النَّظَرِ إِلَى وَجْهِكَ الكَرِيْمِ وَ الشَّوْقَ اِلٰى لِقَآءِك

"O Allah, I ask You for the pleasure of staring at Your beautiful Face and the yearning to meet You."

28

Duʿāʾs for Jannah

How does a person make an appropriate *duʿāʾ* (supplication) for the Afterlife? The answer to this question is actually more complex than it may initially appear at an intuitive level. A careful empirical examination of the Qur'an yields a somewhat astonishing conclusion: only a few verses of the divine scripture contain supplications asking Allah for Paradise. Instead, the bulk of invocations in the Qur'anic corpus require one to seek Allah's mercy or protection from the Hellfire. From this finding one may infer that requesting forgiveness purifies one's inner disposition and allows them to orient themselves towards Allah and the permanent abode of Paradise. With a pure heart, a person will ask Allah for His everlasting Garden, which is the original and true home of humankind. The only requisite criterion is that one supplicate to Allah with a pure and sincere heart. On one occasion, a man went to the Prophet ﷺ and expressed his concern that his *duʿā's* would not be accepted, as they were far too prosaic. He rather bluntly said to the Prophet ﷺ: "I do not understand your humming and the humming of Muʿādh ibn Jabal." With this statement, he was alluding to the eloquent composition of the *duʿā's* formulated by the Prophet ﷺ and Muʿādh ؓ. The Prophet ﷺ asked the man: "What do you do?" In response, he said: "I just recite the *shahādah* (testimony of faith) and then I say:

اللّٰهُمَّ إِنِّي أَسْأَلُكَ الْجَنَّةَ وَأَعُوذُبِكَ مِنَ النَّارِ

'O Allah, I ask You for Paradise and I seek refuge in You from the Fire.'"

The Prophet ﷺ then said to the man: "Both I and Muʿādh say the same." Because this *duʿā'* was approved by the Prophet ﷺ, it comprises the first supplication studied in this chapter. Through his validation, the Prophet ﷺ sought to indicate that simplicity is pivotal when invoking Allah: one should aim to focus on the essential facets of the religion that will serve a person well in the Hereafter.

The second *du'ā'* is an all-inclusive invocation that features in a number of acts of worship. It is found in the following verse of the Qur'an:

رَبَّنَا آتِنَا فِي الدُّنْيَا حَسَنَةً وَفِي الآخِرَةِ حَسَنَةً وَقِنَا عَذَابَ النَّارِ

"Our Lord! Grant us the good of this world and the Hereafter, and protect us from the torment of the Fire."[100]

The great jurist and interpreter al-Ḥasan al-Baṣrī ﷺ explained "the good of this world" segment by stating:

عِلْمًا نَافِعًا وَّرِزْقًا طَيِّبًا وَّعَمَلًا مُّتَقَبَّلًا

"[It refers to asking Allah for] beneficial knowledge, pure sustenance, and accepted deeds."

The goodness of the Hereafter is primarily achieved by avoiding eternal damnation in the Hereafter. Moreover, it refers to the entirety of the domain of Jannah, with its best component being the Beatific Vision. The third supplication is also incidentally found in the Qur'an, which reflects one of the divine promises of Allah:

رَبَّنَا وَآتِنَا مَا وَعَدتَّنَا عَلَىٰ رُسُلِكَ وَلَا تُخْزِنَا يَوْمَ الْقِيٰمَةِ إِنَّكَ لَا تُخْلِفُ الْمِيعَادَ

"Our Lord! Grant us what You have promised us through Your messengers and do not put us to shame on Judgement Day—for certainly You never fail in Your promise."[101]

100 *al-Baqarah*, 201.

101 *Āl 'Imrān*, 194.

O Allah, I ask You
for blessings that never
cease, the coolness of
the eye that never ends,
and for Your pleasure
after Your judgement.
O Allah, I ask You for
Paradise and I seek
refuge in You from
the Fire.

The next supplication has been transmitted via the Prophetic Sunnah. It consists of a lengthy *du'ā'* that the Prophet ﷺ taught the Mother of the Believers 'Ā'ishah ﵂:

اَللَّهُمَّ إِنِّي أَسْأَلُكَ مِنَ الْخَيْرِ كُلِّهِ، عَاجِلِهِ وَآجِلِهِ، مَا عَلِمْتُ مِنْهُ وَمَا لَمْ أَعْلَمْ، وَأَعُوذُ بِكَ مِنَ
الشَّرِّ كُلِّهِ، عَاجِلِهِ وَآجِلِهِ، مَا عَلِمْتُ مِنْهُ وَمَا لَمْ أَعْلَمْ، اَللَّهُمَّ إِنِّي أَسْأَلُكَ مِنْ خَيْرِ مَا سَأَلَكَ
عَبْدُكَ وَنَبِيُّكَ، وَأَعُوذُ بِكَ مِنْ شَرِّ مَا عَاذَ بِهِ عَبْدُكَ وَنَبِيُّكَ، اَللَّهُمَّ إِنِّي أَسْأَلُكَ اَلْجَنَّةَ،
وَمَا قَرَّبَ إِلَيْهَا مِنْ قَوْلٍ أَوْ عَمَلٍ، وَأَعُوذُ بِكَ مِنَ النَّارِ، وَمَا قَرَّبَ مِنْهَا مِنْ قَوْلٍ أَوْ عَمَلٍ،
وَأَسْأَلُكَ أَنْ تَجْعَلَ كُلَّ قَضَاءٍ قَضَيْتَهُ لِي خَيْرًا

"O Allah, I ask You for all that which is good in this world and in the Hereafter, regardless of whether it is what I know or what I do not know. O Allah, I seek refuge with You from all the evil in this world and in Hereafter, regardless of whether it is what I know or what I do not know. O Allah, I ask You for the good that Your slave and Prophet has asked of You, and I seek refuge with You from the evil from which Your slave and Prophet sought refuge from. O Allah, I ask You for Jannah and for that which brings one closer to it, whether in word or deed. And I seek refuge in You from the Hellfire and that which brings one closer to it, whether in word or deed. And I ask You to make every decree that You ordain concerning me good."

The last supplication is also relatively lengthy and found in the Prophetic Sunnah. The Prophet ﷺ taught this *du'ā'* to the noble Companion 'Ammār ibn Yāsir ﵁, who in turn recited it during the Witr prayer. A number of the Successors eventually noticed that 'Ammār was reading a special invocation in this night prayer, and they asked him to recite it to them and reveal its source. 'Ammār ﷺ addressed their concerns by first noting that this *du'ā'* was imparted to him by the Prophet ﷺ, and thereafter proceeded to recite it in full:

اللَّهُمَّ بِعِلْمِكَ الغَيْبَ وَقُدْرَتِكَ عَلَى الخَلْقِ، أَحْيِنِي مَا عَلِمْتَ الحَيَاةَ خَيْرًا لِي، وَتَوَفَّنِي إِذَا
عَلِمْتَ الوَفَاةَ خَيْرًا لِي، اللَّهُمَّ إِنِّي أَسْأَلُكَ خَشْيَتَكَ فِي الغَيْبِ وَالشَّهَادَةِ، وَأَسْأَلُكَ كَلِمَةَ الحَقِّ
فِي الرِّضَا وَالغَضَبِ وَأَسْأَلُكَ القَصْدَ فِي الفَقْرِ وَالغِنَى، وَأَسْأَلُكَ نَعِيمًا لَا يَنْفَدُ، وَأَسْأَلُكَ
قُرَّةَ عَيْنٍ لَا تَنْقَطِعُ، وَأَسْأَلُكَ الرِّضَى بَعْدَ القَضَاءِ، وَأَسْأَلُكَ بَرْدَ العَيْشِ بَعْدَ المَوْتِ،
وَأَسْأَلُكَ لَذَّةَ النَّظَرِ إِلَى وَجْهِكَ وَالشَّوْقَ إِلَى لِقَائِكَ فِي غَيْرِ ضَرَّاءَ مُضِرَّةٍ وَلَا فِتْنَةٍ مُضِلَّةٍ،
اللَّهُمَّ زَيِّنَّا بِزِينَةِ الإِيمَانِ وَاجْعَلْنَا هُدَاةً مُهْتَدِينَ

"O Allah! By Your Knowledge of the Unseen and by Your Power over all creation, let me live if You know that life is good for me, and let me die if You know that death is good for me. O Allah! I ask You to grant me fear of You in both the private and public spheres. And I ask You for the ability to speak a word of truth in times of contentment and anger, and I ask You for moderation in times of wealth and poverty. I ask You for blessings that never cease, the coolness of the eye that never ends, and for Your pleasure after Your judgement. And I ask You for a life of coolness after death, the delight of gazing upon Your noble Face, and the joy of meeting You without any harm or misleading trials befalling me before that. O Allah, adorn us with the beauty of faith, and make us guides who are upon correct guidance."

Every person should aim to learn and memorise a number of these *du'ā's* and ensure to have them recited on a regular basis. That way, they will be able to ensure their attainment of salvation in the Afterlife.

29

The Hidden Rewards in Jannah

Paradise is the realm of unlimited joy and happiness, which ultimately means that its delights and pleasures cannot be properly appreciated in this world of finite dimensions and limited knowledge. As mortal humans living in a temporal world, the main thing that we can know with certainty is that the promise of Allah is true. Moreover, there are a myriad of religious texts which provide vivid descriptions of Paradise in order to increase the longing and aspirations of the believers, with Allah informing His servants that many exotic and awe-inspiring wonders await them. In a brilliant Hadith Qudsī, the Prophet ﷺ related that Allah said: "I have prepared for My righteous slaves what no eye has seen, what no ear has heard, and what no human imagination can possibly grasp." Then the Prophet ﷺ said: "You may recite if you wish:

فَلَا تَعْلَمُ نَفْسٌ مَّآ أُخْفِيَ لَهُم مِّن قُرَّةِ أَعْيُنٍ جَزَآءًۢ بِمَا كَانُوا يَعْمَلُونَ

'No soul can imagine what delights are kept in store for them as a reward for what they used to do.'"[102]

In an authentic Hadith recorded in *Ṣaḥīḥ Muslim*, the Prophet ﷺ said: "Never mind what Allah has told you. What He has not told you is even greater." There are certain pleasures that Allah has intentionally concealed from His friends; such a fact does not in any sense perturb the believers, since they believe in the matters of the Unseen and have firm faith in their Creator's perfect wisdom. In another beautiful Hadith Qudsī, the Prophet ﷺ relates the conversations that Allah has in the Heavenly Court with the Angels after He observes His servants praising Him and seeking His forgiveness. As related by the Prophet ﷺ, notwithstanding His perfect knowledge, He asks the Angels: "What are they asking Me for?" They say: "O Lord, they are asking You for Jannah." He then poses the following question, despite already knowing the answer, "Have they seen Jannah?" In response, they say: "No, O Allah, they have not." Allah then says: "What would the case be if they were to actually see it?" The Angels state: "They would be even more eager for it. And they would beseech You with even more sincerity."

---

102 *al-Sajdah*, 17.

A number of pivotal spiritual lessons can be derived from this report. First, it provides a vivid description of how Allah boasts to the Angels of how His select servants from the believers love and seek His pleasure. The decisive evidence that Allah provides to justify this conclusion is that the believers ask Allah for Paradise, despite never having the opportunity to see it directly. Secondly, the report confirms that a Muslim does not need to actually see and perceive Paradise in order to become an obedient servant and connect with the Creator. In fact, at a somewhat paradoxical level, limited knowledge of a being or concept adds a layer of mystery and causes one to be attracted to them more intensively. For instance, Allah only disclosed a limited number of His divine names in this world, and will only reveal the rest in the Hereafter. Likewise, He only provided the names of a few levels and stations of Paradise, with the rest remaining undisclosed. This is similar to the notion of how there are 100 dimensions of mercy created by Allah, but only one of them is existent in this world. Such reports inspire the believers to perform acts of goodness and lead moral lives in the hope that they will be showered with Allah's mercy—which will be amplified with the remaining 99 unknown forms—in the Afterlife.

These aforementioned narrations inspire us to seek the forgiveness of Allah and lead our lives with a blank slate. Thankfully, there is a beautiful *duʿāʾ* which the Prophet ﷺ taught his ummah that can erase one's sins and cause them to be forgiven. This special and powerful invocation bears the eminent title of Sayyid al-Istighfār (The Chief of Seeking Forgiveness), and it should be recited on a regular basis. This short but powerful invocation consists of the following formula:

اللَّهُمَّ أَنْتَ رَبِّي لَا إِلَهَ إِلَّا أَنْتَ خَلَقْتَنِي وَأَنَا عَبْدُكَ وَأَنَا عَلَى عَهْدِكَ وَوَعْدِكَ مَا اسْتَطَعْتُ،
أَعُوذُ بِكَ مِنْ شَرِّ مَا صَنَعْتُ، أَبُوءُ لَكَ بِنِعْمَتِكَ عَلَيَّ، وَأَبُوءُ لَكَ بِذَنْبِي
فَاغْفِرْ لِي فَإِنَّهُ لَا يَغْفِرُ الذُّنُوبَ إِلَّا أَنْتَ

"O Allah, You are my Lord. There is no God but You. You created me and I am Your slave. I am exerting my best efforts to fulfil the covenant that I have taken from You, and I seek refuge in You from the sins that I have committed. I acknowledge the grand favours that You have showered upon me, and I likewise acknowledge all my faults and shortcomings. So, forgive me, for no one forgives sins except for You."

After relating this beautiful supplication, the Prophet ﷺ said: "Whoever makes this *du'ā'* during the day with firm belief in it and then dies on the same day before the evening, he will be one of the inhabitants of Jannah. And if he makes this *du'ā'* during the evening with firm belief in it and then dies before the morning, he will be one of the dwellers of Jannah." If one carefully evaluates this *du'ā'*, they will find that it revolves around the notion of forgiveness and the removal of sins. This is, in fact, a fundamental theme of the Qur'an, since the primary barriers that bar one's entrance into Paradise consist of sins and moral lapses; if these shortcomings are pardoned, one's entry into Jannah can be guaranteed.

But the effective mechanism which allows one to qualify for Allah's mercy does not have to necessarily be a supplication. It can, in fact, be a righteous deed that is performed with a sincere heart. It could be an act that is deemed small and trivial from the viewpoint of the doer, yet unbeknownst to them it is the decisive factor that causes them to become a *walī* (friend of the divine) of Allah. Regarding the hidden effects of pious actions, ʿAlī ibn Abī Ṭālib ﷺ said: "Allah has concealed two things within two things. He has concealed His *awliyā'* (friends of the Divine) amongst His regular servants." In other words, a person who is presumed to be a scholarly individual in this world may be a despised figure in the sight of Allah, whilst a normal layperson can be deemed a *walī* due to their acts of piety. ʿAlī ﷺ then mentioned the second undisclosed article by stating: "And Allah has concealed His *riḍā* (pleasure) within his good deeds." One can thus not know which of their deeds are pleasing to Allah; as such, they should aim to perform as many good deeds as possible to earn the contentment of their Creator.

In a parallel fashion, the great gnostic Ibn ʿAṭā'allāh al-Iskandarī ﷺ expressed a beautiful *ḥikmah* (aphorism) regarding how human reason lacks the ability to appreciate the divine promises of Allah and why the divine recompense for one's deeds cannot be allotted in this temporal world.

In this pithy yet conceptually-rich maxim, the Imam said:

إِنَّمَا جَعَلَ الدَّارَ الآخِرَةَ مَحَلًّا لِجَزَاءِ عِبَادِهِ الْمُؤْمِنِينَ لِأَنَّ هَذِهِ الدَّارَ لَا تَسَعُ مَا يُرِيدُ
أَنْ يُعْطِيَهُمْ وَلِأَنَّهُ أَجَلَّ أَقْدَارَهُمْ عَنْ أَنْ يُجَازِيَهُمْ فِي دَارٍ لَا بَقَاءَ لَهَا

"The Hereafter has been rendered the permanent abode for recompensing the believing servants since this temporal world cannot encompass what He desires to give them. And He has honoured their ranks exceedingly, such that He would not wish to confer His reward in a transient abode."

Instead of allotting the rewards of the believers prematurely in a perishable realm like this world, Allah will store their treasures, palaces, and gardens in a permanent abode found in the Afterlife.

(It will be said to the believers)

"Enter (Jannah) in peace and security."

AL-ḤIJR, 46

30

Your Only Regret in Jannah

Humans are fallible and deficient beings, and the pious believers are no exception to this rule. There are many moments where they may experience lapses or fail to connect with Allah at the optimal level. But for the pious friends of Allah, even the inability to meet the ideal standard of conduct with the Creator of the cosmos is deemed a deficiency. This is because when one develops an intense connection and relationship with their Lord, the slightest dereliction of duty causes them to feel discomfort. In a similar fashion to how the greatest pleasure of Paradise is the Beatific Vision, the best experience in this world is becoming a close and intimate servant of Allah, whereby one's happiness is solely tied to following His decrees. This God-centred philosophy can be appreciated by reading a moving statement issued by Abū al-Dardā' ﷺ on his deathbed: "Were it not for the existence of three things, I would not have been able to live in this world." With this comment, Abū al-Dardā' ﷺ was pointing to how there were three matters which made the worldly life bearable. Upon perusing this statement, many individuals might presume that these distinctive things would be solely material in nature, that is, physical possessions or individuals that made his life pleasurable. However, in actual fact, the three matters in question were the following: "The joy of spending a hot summer noon dehydrated due to fasting that day, the joy of prostrating before Allah in the latter parts of the night, and the joy of sitting in the companionship of pious people whose discourses are replete with points of wisdom and reflections, just like the fruits from a luscious garden." After assessing the biography of Abū al-Dardā' ﷺ, one will find that this noble Companion spent his entire life engrossed in the worship of Allah, and his only joy was conversing with Allah during his prayer and fasting. We should all strive to emulate this golden example by ensuring that our acts of worship are performed with full devotion and reverence to Allah. That way, we can depart from this world whilst knowing that we discharged our religious responsibilities in the best manner possible. The same theme is articulated by other pious predecessors as well.

For instance, on one occasion the students of ʿAbdullāh ibn Masʿūd ؓ sought clarification concerning the meaning of the following Qur'anic verse:

وَ لَا تَحْسَبَنَّ الَّذِيْنَ قُتِلُوْا فِيْ سَبِيْلِ اللّٰهِ اَمْوَاتًا بَلْ اَحْيَآءٌ عِنْدَ رَبِّهِمْ يُرْزَقُوْنَ

"Never think of those martyred in the cause of Allah as dead. In fact, they are alive with their Lord, well provided for."[103]

ʿAbdullāh ibn Masʿūd ؓ responded by relating the following Hadith from the Prophet ﷺ: "The souls of the *shuhadā'* (martyrs) live in the bodies of green birds and they have their nests in chandeliers hung from the Throne of the Almighty. They eat from the fruits of Paradise whenever and wherever they wish, and then they comfortably rest within these chandeliers. Their Lord then gazes upon them and asks: 'Do you wish to have anything?' In response, they state: 'O Lord, what more can we desire? We already eat from the fruits of Paradise wherever we like.' Yet, Allah will pose the same question three more times. After noticing that Allah is unwavering in His request, they say, 'O Lord, we wish that You could return our souls to our bodies so that we could be slain in Your way over and over again.' Upon noticing that they have no other need beyond that, they are left in their state of bliss."

Moreover, in another Hadith, the Prophet ﷺ said: "No one who enters Paradise will wish to return once more to this world, even if he could be granted everything on Earth.

---

103 *Āl ʿImrān*, 169.

The only exception is the *shahīd* (martyr), for they will wish to be returned to this world and be slain 10 additional times for the sake of Allah." Such a wish does not in any manner reflect a desire for violence or torment. Instead, these martyrs are touched and moved by Allah's mercy in the Afterlife, with their love towards Him being amplified so immensely that they desire to sacrifice themselves once more. The concept of sacrifice is a fundamental tenet that is found in many religious texts. In fact, the Messenger of Allah ﷺ once said: "I would love to be a *shahīd* in the cause of Allah and be resurrected again, then become a *shahīd* and be resurrected once more, and then be resurrected further and become a *shahīd* again."

The love for sacrificing one's life and prized possessions for the sake of Allah is a hallmark of the believers, since they know that they will be handsomely recompensed in the Hereafter. Unlike the regret of the people of Hellfire, the regret of the believers will not be that they failed to attain a station in Paradise. Instead, because they love Allah so intensely, they will lament the fact that they could not serve Him at the level He truly deserves. Since He is the Creator of the cosmos and every particle found in this Universe, no one will be able to repay Allah for the blessings and bounties He allotted them during their lifetime.

O Allah, we ask You for our eternal home in Jannah and we seek refuge in You from the Fire. We yearn to meet You and to gain the pleasure of staring at Your beautiful Face in the everlasting Gardens with our beloved Prophet ﷺ and the righteous, together with our loved ones.

Āmīn.

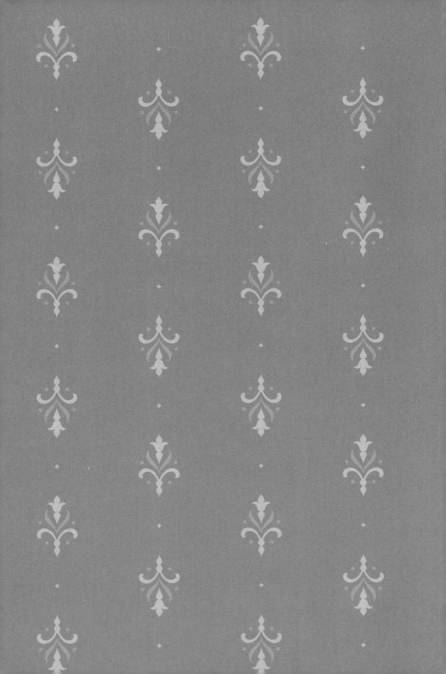